13 Jan 68

To Jean-Paul

from your old
Air Force Buddy,

Keith Campbell

IN CANADIAN SKIES

FRANK H. ELLIS

50 YEARS of
ADVENTURE and PROGRESS
IN CANADIAN SKIES

*Endorsed fully by
the National Co-ordinating Council
for the Golden Anniversary of
Flight in Canada*

THE RYERSON PRESS ~ TORONTO

Published 1959

NOTE

Photos of R.C.A.F.'s "Golden Hawks" precision
acrobatic team are reproduced on jacket by
courtesy of the Department of National Defence

PRINTED AND BOUND IN CANADA
BY THE RYERSON PRESS, TORONTO

TO
THE PILOTS AND
ENGINEERS WHOSE EFFORTS
MADE THIS
B
O
O
K
POSSIBLE

GERVAIS

Foreword

FROM THE DAY an airplane first flew in Canada, on February 23, 1909, aerial adventure and progress have travelled forward, hand in hand.

Since that time, hundreds of thousands of pilots and airplanes have flown in Canada, on innumerable missions.

From among them all, certain exploits stand out to a higher degree above the majority, and some airplanes have become just a little more famous, due to their flying abilities or because of some particular feat accomplished by them.

It is to honour such pilots, and aircraft, that the true stories contained in this book have been gathered together, to form a compact and accurate little history of their own.

No matter what the nationality of the pilots involved, or in what country the airplane had its origin, if the exploit is worthy beyond ordinary mention it has found a place in this book.

When reading about these aerial highlights connected with Canadian air history, it is an excellent idea to have a world atlas handy, and to open it at the map, or maps, relating to the geographical areas which are mentioned.

Much added enjoyment can be gained in this manner as in imagination you go along on such flying journeys to settlements in the Canadian northland or perhaps to or from distant countries.

"Fly with the pilots" to the Arctic or over Greenland's icy mountains, or maybe to destinations or starting points in Europe or South America.

It may come as quite a surprise to many Canadians to learn that such far-away places long ago came closer to Canadian centres through the progress of flight.

Foreign lands are ever coming nearer and nearer, in point of travel time, as faster and faster airliners speed on their varied routes to and from most parts of the world.

The tremendous advance made by modern, all-metal aircraft over the old-time, wood and wire flying machines is continually going forward to higher achievement. Even so, let us not forget or overlook the names of the men and the women, and of course the airplanes, which played such vital roles in the formation of our aerial history.

The adventures, attainments and progress in the air which have taken place in Canada in the past fifty years have been spectacular in some instances and practically unknown in others.

Combined, it all adds up to one thing, a wonderful tradition in the air which is unrivalled by any other country on earth.

FRANK H. ELLIS.

Contents

Part
one / CANADIAN FLYING BEGINS

1. Dr. Bell's Hopes
Come True

FOR CENTURIES MEN have designed and built a variety of strange-looking contraptions with which they hoped to accomplish sustained flight, and they did so for good reason.

History proves beyond doubt that human beings have always envied the free flight of birds, and with queer-built apparatus many tried, and others died, in futile efforts.

Then at last it was done. The world learned that the Wright brothers had flown their power-driven airplane at Kitty Hawk, North Carolina, on December 17, 1903, and their success stirred experimenters everywhere to renewed efforts.

True, pioneer flying machines were queer-looking things, but often enough their puny looks belied the fact that they were well designed, and that they flew well.

The men and women who flew them were a courageous lot, although the general public considered all of them to be touched in the head. Even so, they were all true explorers, setting off on dangerous missions into the unknown air, and when they did so in their pioneer machines their lives hung in the balance. Success came only with sheer ability and the nerve to carry it through.

Canadians early took part in such work and earned an honoured place in pioneer aviation, and in the years which have followed a splendid tradition has been formed.

During the early years of flight, the main centres of population in Canada were situated widely apart, and although considerable flying took place in the Dominion before the outbreak of World War One, much of it did not then become general knowledge.

Information relating to Canadians who built and flew their own pioneer planes suffered much the same fate, although some certainly deserved much better.

Of them all, the most prominent by far were the men who organized the Aerial Experiment Association and who were instrumental in discovering many solutions to successful flight during the pioneer era.

They were the first Canadians to fly and they established outstanding air history.

The first meagre news that Canadians were interested in airplanes, and were willing to spend money building them, became news in the fall of 1907. It originated from Baddeck, a tiny maritime village on Cape Breton Island, which is a part of Nova Scotia. The brief news item divulged that Alexander Graham Bell, inventor of the telephone, was to head the undertaking.

It was not an entirely new project for him, as he had been interested in the possibility of flight by man for many years. In an effort to learn something of the problems involved, he had designed and made many large kites of varying sizes and shapes.

During the late summer of 1907, he discussed the possibilities of building a man-carrying airplane with two young Canadians who were his guests at his beautiful home at Baddeck. They were Frederick "Casey" Baldwin and John A. D. McCurdy, both of whom had that year graduated from engineering studies at the University of Toronto.

Their talk centred on the design of a suitable craft, and how to go about making it. It was then that Mrs. Bell took an interest in their discussion, and offered to finance the undertaking if they wished to go ahead with it.

Thus in a peaceful Canadian maritime village the Aerial Experiment Association was formed with the avowed intention of building a motor-driven airplane which would carry a man in full flight.

As an engine to power it was a prime necessity, Dr. Bell got in touch with a man he knew who might do the job and who had a motorcycle workshop at Hammondsport, New York. He was Glenn H. Curtiss, and because his small factory was well established, and he signified his willingness to help, Dr. Bell decided to carry out all constructional work at Hammondsport.

Things were quickly organized, and the building of the first machine got under way. Three additional airplanes later were made by the group, and they became world renowned as a consequence.

When the first craft was completed, they named it the *Red Wing*, doing so because of the colouring of all its silk-covered surfaces. The 40 h.p. air-cooled engine Curtiss designed and made, was installed, and they were ready for tests.

The swift-moving times in which we now live have pushed many memorable events into the background, to linger mislaid and almost forgotten. One of these exploits was the first flight of the *Red Wing*, at Hammondsport, March 12, 1908.

It was a splendid pioneer flying episode, and all Canadians should be proud of "Casey" Baldwin, who was the pilot. He was not only the first Canadian to fly an airplane—quite an achievement in itself—but he was also the first British subject to do so, anywhere in the world.

Like his namesake made famous in song, the "Casey" Jones of railroad renown, Baldwin also pushed a throttle lever wide open to achieve everlasting fame but he had no steel tracks to follow, his rush through space was in the trackless air.

A fourth young man admitted to the organization was Lieut. Thomas Selfridge, who was attached to the Association through a request from the United States government to Dr. Bell.

The frozen surface of Lake Keuka, near Hammondsport, made a perfect area from which to conduct experiments. To suit the occasion, a sleigh type of undergear was designed and fitted to the *Red Wing* instead of wheels.

Residents of the surrounding area already knew of the goings-on and had become highly interested as the work on the first airplane neared completion. When the news began to circulate that the craft was completed, and that tests were to be made, a large crowd gathered on the ice to witness the event. Many of them brought along their ice-skates.

The seat upon which Baldwin sat had presented no difficulty in manufacture.   It was simply an ordinary kitchen chair, with the legs sawn off, fitted to the machine just ahead of the lower wing, and in the centre.

A pointed "nose," covered with red silk, was the pilot's "cockpit."   After squeezing his athletic figure into its narrow confines, Baldwin perched himself on the seat and the engine was started.   As he pushed the throttle wide open, the hum broke into a roar and the *Red Wing* began to move over the ice, quickly speeding up to a fast clip.

With his heart beating wildly with elation, "Casey" held tight to the controls, and as he almost unconsciously pulled back on the column he felt the wings lift, and was flying free.

Perhaps no one there that day was more completely astonished than Baldwin when the 420-lb. craft lifted from the ice so smoothly and quickly.   As he saw the ice rushing past below and felt the wind beating against his face, he knew that he and his fellow builders had managed to make a plane that could carry a man in full flight.

Numerous spectators set off after him across the ice, their skates flashing in the sunlight, and they were not far behind the airman when he shut off the engine and made a good landing, after having flown a distance of 319 feet.

After its first triumph, the *Red Wing* was destined to fly only once again before it was damaged too badly for repairs to be undertaken.   At the end of a second flight, a few days later, Baldwin had covered a distance of 120 feet when a gust of wind caught one wing and smashed it against the ice.   In the resultant mix-up the craft was badly wrecked, but "Casey" suffered no ill effect.

In turn, the Association built three additional airplanes, all slightly different in design but improving in airworthiness, as the young designers learned their various lessons by trial and error.

The second machine was named the *White Wing*, then came the *June Bug* and finally the *Silver Dart*. All of them made their initial flying tests at Hammondsport at a nearby racetrack.

Some excellent flights were made in the *June Bug* by Curtiss and by McCurdy. The former pilot earned a top American prize by flying it for a distance of over one kilometre on July 4, 1908, to win the *Scientific American Trophy* for being the first man to fly such a distance in the western hemisphere.

When the winter of 1908-1909 set in Dr. Bell decided that at least one of the Association's "flying machines" should make its debut in Canada. With this laudable object in view, he had the *Silver Dart* sent by rail and ship from Hammondsport to Baddeck, in January, 1909. It was then assembled at the Nova Scotia village in readiness for the historical event.

As nearby Bras d'Or Lake was solidly frozen over, offering a smooth area for the job, plans were made to make the flight in February. The machine was fitted with wheels, not with sleighs, as had been the *Red Wing*. But as taking off from, and landing on, ice was much the same as smooth ground, no change in the landing gear was required.

On February 23rd, Dr. Bell's cherished wish came true when John McCurdy took the *Dart* off the ice and flew it for almost one mile.

So he, too, joined his friend Baldwin for entry in the book of everlasting fame by becoming the first person to fly an airplane at any point in the Dominion of Canada.

In later years, when flying records became better classified, McCurdy was to receive greater recognition. Not only was it established that his was the first flight in Canada, but also that he was the first British subject to make a successfully controlled flight in a heavier-than-air machine at any point in the British Empire.

On February 23, 1959, a ceremony took place at Baddeck in connection with the celebrations marking the fiftieth anniversary of powered flight in Canada. It resulted in a widely publicized affair, and was attended by many celebrities and spectators, the guest of honour being Mr. John A. D. McCurdy in person.

A full-sized replica of the *Silver Dart* had been constructed due to the initiative and diligence of Leading Aircraftsman Lionel McCaffrey, who did a splendid job with the aid of other R.C.A.F. personnel at Trenton, Ontario.

Wing Commander Paul Hartman of the R.C.A.F. had the difficult task of flying the craft in a high wind, and he did famously for the first portion of the flight over the ice-covered surface of Lake Bras d'Or, just as McCurdy had done, fifty years before.

When a wild gust of wind caught the fragile craft and carried it up to 100 feet, the pilot brought it under control again in masterly fashion, but a second gust stronger than the first smashed at it again. The left wing tip struck the ice with force and the entire machine was hurled to the ice, damaging it quite severely, and wrecking the left wing and undergear, but fortunately the pilot stepped out of the debris uninjured.

Going one better than the original flight accomplished in 1909, a number of special letters were carried on the short hop, being sent by Prime Minister Diefenbaker addressed to H.M. Queen Elizabeth, and the heads of the British, United States and French governments. On each envelope was affixed one of the new five-cent postage stamps designed specially by the Postal Department to mark the great event. The stamps went on sale throughout Canada on the same date.

It was the first time in history that any country in the world had been able to celebrate its Golden Jubilee of powered flight with an exact flying replica of the original machine used, and to have the pioneer pilot who flew it there in person. It was a great day, and casts tremendous credit on all those who had a part in its origination, and in its fulfilment.

2. A Western Pioneer

WILLIAM WALLACE GIBSON was brought up as a child on a prairie farm some miles from Regina.   As there were no schools within many miles of the homestead, his chief duty as a boy was to ride herd over the few head of cattle his parents owned. His only playmates were Indian children from the nearby Piapot Reserve, the head of which was venerable Chief Kisikaw Wawasam, a name which literally translated means "Flash-in-the-Sky Boy."

One day when William was playing with the grandson of the aged Chief, the elderly Cree patted him on the head and said, "Some day when you have grown up, you, too, will be a great chief."

The words made a deep impression on Gibson, and he had good reasons for remembering them many years later.

William loved to make and fly kites, and became very adept at doing so.   Often he rode his pony at the gallop across the open land, trailing a high-flying kite behind just for the pleasure of seeing it fly.

As he grew up Gibson became a prosperous farmer.   Good crops enabled him to establish credit at the bank, and he branched out to become the owner of three flourishing general stores in nearby centres.   The largest was at the village of Balgonie, fifteen miles east of Regina.

When the news reached him in 1903 that the Wright brothers had flown, he became keenly interested and began experimenting with model airplanes of his own design.   The first he built were fashioned from paper and odds and ends of wood. As he progressed he powered some with elastic bands, which drove a hand-carved propeller.

Later, he devised a "motor" from the spring of an ordinary window-blind roller. Although his only knowledge of free flight was guesswork, based on ideas gleaned from his kite-flying experiments, he finally constructed a large model airplane which flew and was very stable in the air.

At daybreak, one Sunday morning in June, 1904, from the rooftop of his Balgonie store, he gave it its first test. The small plane took off at a fast clip, crossing high over the street, and headed for the distant railway tracks. There it struck the top of a stationary railway box-car, and toppled out of sight on the other side.

Later the same Sunday the local physician, Doctor Kaulb-fleisch, dropped in to have a chat with Gibson. During the conversation a twinkle came into the doctor's eyes when he remarked, "You know, Bill, when I drove into the village very early this morning, after attending the Morgans' baby on their farm, I wondered what kind of a funny bird that was you were trying to catch on your rooftop." Gibson said not a word, so the doctor continued, "I never saw one like it before. You know, it flew right over my buggy and lit in the grass by the station."

The cat was out of the bag all right, but Gibson prevailed on the physician to keep the secret. Only the doctor and one or two other friends of Gibson ever learned at that time what he was up to. In later years, Gibson said he asked them to keep quiet because he did not wish to have his banker think he was a bit loose in the head.

So encouraged was Gibson by his experiments that he decided to design and build an airplane large enough to carry a man. But to ensure as much privacy as possible he started his project on his farm, four miles south of the village.

His first major objective was to make an engine, and it was well under way when the 1905 railroad-building boom swept through that part of Saskatchewan. Gibson caught the fever.

In the hope of making pots of money he signed a contract to lay down twenty miles of right-of-way for the Grand Trunk Pacific. Later he took on a similar contract to construct twenty miles more.

A complete novice at such business, he was unable to meet various time clauses and, as he later ruefully expressed it, "Instead of cleaning up a lot of money, the banks cleaned me up." To pay forfeits and construction deficits he was forced to sell his three stores. Altogether he lost $40,000.

Twenty-seven years of age at the time, Gibson lost interest in farming and the prairies. So with his wife and small family he moved to Victoria, British Columbia, after making arrangements to rent his farm.

While trying to establish himself in the coastal city in 1907, he met a man named Locky Grant who was broke but the owner of a gold claim at Elk River, on Vancouver Island.

Becoming interested in Locky's offer to sell, Gibson purchased a seventeen-foot boat with a single-cylinder engine, and with Locky set off to inspect the claim. On a map the route looked peaceful enough. He expected no difficulties, but he soon learned the difference between the sea on a map and actuality. The eight days it took to reach Elk River were packed full of adventure and near disasters and became a story in itself.

Once there, Gibson thought the claim looked good, although he had never seen one in his life before. He became the new owner. He and Grant worked it for the entire summer, and eventually returned to Victoria with gold valued at $1,000. With such proof Gibson was able to sell the claim to a mining syndicate for $10,000.

With plenty of cash now to urge him on, Gibson at once put his energies to designing a full-sized airplane, and a new engine to power it. The work began in 1908, with every part having to be made by hand, entirely to his own plans. Gibson had never received a single lesson in either drafting or engineering, so where his skill came from is hard to guess, but his fertile brain enabled him to overcome all difficulties.

Victoria was about the last place on earth where materials for building an airplane were readily available. His friends openly scoffed at his efforts. Mere acquaintances, meeting him on the street, would spread out their arms full length and go through the motions of flapping them like wings, as they walked past.

Yet Gibson persisted. After making a number of large models and testing them from the crest of nearby Beacon Hill Park, he chose the one which showed the best all-round performance, and drew plans from it for a full-sized machine. He also laboriously worked out details for a six-cylinder engine, which proved to be a very unorthodox idea. It was to operate on a two-cycle firing principle instead of the then generally accepted four-cycle type. It was also planned to be air-cooled.

When he took the blueprints to a local machine shop Dan Hutchinson, the manager, took one look at them, threw up his hands and almost screamed, "That thing won't work." However, the inventor was adamant. He wanted it made exactly the way he had planned it, so reluctantly, the firm went to work on the job.

Gibson was a remarkable man all right. When the engine was completed, it ran smoothly and developed approximately 50 h.p. although it weighed only 210 lbs. As history was later to record, his six-cylinder engine was the first successful airplane motor ever fabricated in Canada. Today it may be seen on permanent display in the Aeronautical Museum, established by the National Research Council at Ottawa, where it is one of their most prized exhibits.

Gibson's entire airplane was finished by the late summer of 1910, and he named it the *Gibson Twin-plane*.

The engine was installed in the centre of the main framework, which was fashioned from two well-braced booms of fir wood. The craft was quite unique for that period, because the engine operated two propellers, *one behind the other*, each coupled close to the engine, fore and aft.

Two large wings were attached to the main framework, one at the front and one at the rear. The landing-gear, or what was then termed the running-gear, consisted of four bicycle wheels suitably mounted below the main frame. Probably the strangest single piece of equipment was the pilot's seat. Gibson used an ordinary horse saddle for that, stripped down to save as much weight as possible.

At last the long-awaited day came when the machine was completed, and it was moved from its shed in the heart of Victoria to a farm near Mount Tolmie, several miles north of the city. Transportation was made with the aid of a team-drawn wagon.

The air was full of tension on September 8, 1910, when Gibson made his first test, but it ended up a disappointing day because the running-gear buckled, resulting in a delay of further tests until the 24th.

The fragile-looking flying machine was housed in a large tent while repairs were made, and peeping Toms from the surrounding area abounded. A great air of expectancy, mingled with doubt, could be seen on the faces of the spectators who stood by as the *Twin-plane* was wheeled from its tent on the 24th, and Gibson climbed up to take his seat on the leather saddle.

Excitement ran high. The budding airman expressed the hope of flying across the Gulf of Georgia all the way to Vancouver, in an endeavour to collect a bet he had made. Why Gibson expected to win the wager is clear enough, because he certainly had faith in his machine. But what the result would be was anyone's guess.

The lusty roar of the engine shattered the calm of that autumn morning, and as soon as Gibson was satisfied it was operating at full strength he raised his hand as a signal to his helpers to let go their hold of the craft.

A gentle dawn breeze was blowing across the field as the *Twin-plane* sped over the grass, and almost instantly it lifted gracefully into the air. Reporters, whom Gibson had wisely invited to be on hand, stood amazed at seeing their first airplane in flight, and a cheer went up as the machine began to climb.

Thrilled with the exhilaration of speed and actual flight, Gibson yet had clearness of mind to notice that the airplane was drifting off course, although at the time he did not realize it was the wind that was causing it.

In an effort to continue straight down the field the fledgling pilot made a bad mistake. The rudder lines, attached to a leather belt around his chest, were quite easy to operate, but by mischance Gibson leaned to the wrong side, and the *Twin-plane* veered off course more than ever.

By this time the group of watchers up-field were on tiptoes as they saw the drama unfold. Unable to help, they just held their breath and waited. The end was not long in coming. Like Gibson they, too, saw the large stand of oak trees which lay right in his path. With quick presence of mind, the airman switched off the motive power and made a splendid landing, but he had no control of the craft once it was on the ground. The machine rolled on at speed and finally, like Don Quixote charging the windmill, the dainty aircraft performed a similar act.

Setting its nose at a particularly sturdy oak, it charged full tilt. There was a great sound of crackling wood and the front of the *Twin-plane* disintegrated in a flash as it struck the immovable tree.

Maybe if the stirrups had been left on the saddle they might have helped Gibson to keep his seat, but without them he did not have a chance. Like a jockey whose mount has baulked at a jump, Gibson rose into the air on a free flight of his own, to end up yards ahead of the wreckage as he skidded on his chest to a stop. His hurts were much less physical than mental. Although he was bruised and shaken up, the pain which hurt him the worst was the sight of his beloved *Twin-plane*, forlorn and shattered.

Measurements showed that the distance he had flown was approximately 200 feet. Compared with other first flights of that period this was very good indeed. Even a hundred feet with an entirely new type of airplane was considered quite an accomplishment.

The first airplane flight ever made by man, when Orville Wright flew at Kitty Hawk, North Carolina, in December, 1903, carried him only 120 feet. The first flight ever made in England, by A. V. Roe, in June, 1908, was less than a hundred. Santos Dumont, who was the first person to fly an airplane anywhere in the eastern hemisphere when he flew in France in 1906, travelled only 200 feet. It is obvious therefore that, for his day, William Gibson's flight was no mean feat.

Once he had tasted the thrill of flight, nothing could restrain him from further experiments. To raise money to make this possible he sold his home in Victoria, and continued with little delay.

During the time the *Twin-plane* was nearing completion, Gibson had obtained a book written by the famous British inventor, Sir Hiram Maxim. In its pages were fully outlined numerous theories and experiments relating to the use of narrow multiple wings for use on an airplane.

Gibson was so impressed with Maxim's treatise, he considered them better than his own ideas. So he redesigned his original aircraft to conform with the new suggestions, and the final result was the *Gibson Multi-plane.*

He used the same engine from the *Twin-plane,* but fitted it with a single propeller which replaced the original two. It proved much more satisfactory by developing more forward thrust.

The many narrow "wings" which he incorporated in the design of his second plane were all fashioned entirely by hand, from laminated spruce wood. The wings of orthodox airplanes of that period were all covered with a cloth material of some nature, but not so the *Multi-plane.* There was not one single square inch of fabric in its entire make-up.

Instead of metal hinges for use on the rudder, ailerons and the front elevator, the inventor used strips of leather. He was nothing if not original.

When the strange machine was completed by late spring of 1911, it looked for all the world like a glorified "pulled-down" venetian blind.

As Gibson wanted to get away from the oak trees, he arranged to conduct initial experiments of the new aircraft at Ladner, British Columbia, on a farm the then Lieutenant-Governor of the Province, Honourable Thomas Paterson, owned and placed at his disposal.

A long spell of wet weather delayed tests so much that arrangements were finally made to ship the *Multi-plane* by rail to a friend's farm near Calgary, Alberta, where climatic conditions were expected to be better.

Before the plane was shipped over the mountains it was placed on exhibition in a "Made-in-Canada" fair, being held in July at Vancouver's Hastings Park. While there it stole the show.

By flight test time, Mrs. Gibson had become alarmed for her husband's safety, so she extracted a promise from him that he would not endeavour to fly the machine himself. One of Gibson's helpers, Alex Japp, cheerfully took over the risky job and thus unknowingly became Canada's first hired test pilot.

After reaching the farm near Calgary and being rigged, the *Multi-plane* underwent a number of tests. Several short hops were accomplished, and it proved itself to be completely airworthy. Then came the announcement that a full flight test would be made on August 12, 1911.

Reporters from the Calgary *Herald* and the *Telegram*, together with city dignitaries, were invited to be on hand and before their astonished eyes the "Gibson flying machine" took off on schedule with Japp at the controls. Later measurements proved that it flew for almost one mile at a height of approximately 100 feet.

As the excited spectators pounded after it afoot across the prairie the sound from its engine suddenly ceased, and they drew up to watch what appeared to be the beginning of a good landing. Suddenly, as the craft touched down, there came the sound of splintering wood, and a great cloud of dust billowed lazily into the air.

When the small crowd of people finally reached the wreckage, it was to find Japp ruefully rubbing various parts of his bruised anatomy, but happily enough he was not seriously injured. The same could not be said for the *Multi-plane*. It lay a tangled heap of wreckage, shattered beyond repair. Asked what had happened, Japp pointed to the area all around and stated briefly, "Badger holes."

He went on to say that when he had decided he had flown far enough, he shut off the motor to glide down to a landing, but too late saw the area was pitted with badger holes in all directions. Even a modern plane could scarcely land in that rough stuff without suffering some damage, and it was fatal for the *Multi-plane*.

It was a bad day for Gibson, too. With his money almost gone and a wife and family depending on him, he was obliged to give up aircraft experiments and bow to defeat. So aviation lost a promising personality for all time.

During a holiday at Regina in July, 1948, Gibson had good reason to remember an episode of his youth. At a colourful ceremony attended by government officials and members of the Royal Canadian Mounted Police, together with many Indians from various reservations, Gibson was installed as a Chief of the Cree Nations. The small boy, who had been his playmate so many years before, had now become the Chief of the Piapot Reserve. It was he who presented to Gibson the Eagle Feather Headdress of the tribe, together with a ceremonial blanket and a long-stemmed council-pipe.

The ceremony invested in Gibson a full chieftainship in the Cree Nations, but the real highlight of the affair for him surely rested in the title they bestowed upon him. To his great satisfaction he was named Chief Kisikaw Wawasam, the same rank which had belonged to the venerated Chief who had patted his head so many years before. With signal and appropriate thoughtfulness his Indian friends had honoured him with the name of "Flash-in-the-Sky Boy."

So Indian lore came to be woven into the pattern of pioneer flying in Canada, regardless of the fact that the men who made it possible were of different races and lived in worlds apart.

3. A Young Man of Nerve

YOUNG LARRY LESH originally hailed from Chicago, but went to Canada when his parents moved to Montreal in 1906. In his early teens at the time, Larry soon was installed as a student at the Peel Street School. He was a good pupil, but his thoughts were equally divided between learning his lessons and his great ambition to fly gliders.

During the year prior to leaving Chicago his mother and father had allowed him to construct a number of full-sized properly-designed gliders, which were capable of lifting his weight into the air. They had also granted him permission to be towed aloft in them.

They would never have done this if it had not been for one important influence. The world-famous glider pilot, Octave Chanute, was a close friend of the family. He promised to coach Larry in making his gliders and in the safety of flying them. So Mr. and Mrs. Lesh willingly gave their consent, allowing their son to venture into the air.

By the time Larry moved to Canada he had made several glider flights under the watchful eyes of Mr. Chanute. All of them were in gliders he had made himself from designs given to him by Mr. Chanute. An automobile was used to tow the gliders to get them into the air.

In Montreal, Larry continued with his experiments on a farm near Dominion Park, but his towing "apparatus" shrank to one horsepower. In fact, it had four feet, and was a horse. A teen-age friend sat astride the animal to urge it to greater effort as it galloped across the wide acres of a pasture, the taut towrope being attached to the rear of the saddle.

Once airborne, Larry would cast the towrope adrift when he had gained about 75 feet in height, and many times he accomplished free flights of distances averaging 250 feet. With each one he became a little more adept, but landings were always a tricky business. They required fine judgment and considerable athletic ability. They were made at a run on Larry's own two sturdy legs while his hands and arms clung to the lightweight glider to prevent it striking the ground.

By midsummer of 1907, he had built another glider of Chanute type to which he added a few items of his design. The chief improvements were small movable flaps at the ends of the top wing. He found, in later tests, that their manipulation during flight added greatly to control and stability. Another idea was a small tail section attached to the main planes by a single boom. By moving the apparatus up or down, or from side to side, perfect control in the air resulted. This was a big step ahead from the original flight-control methods, which could only be effected by swinging the body in desired directions to retain balance when the glider inadvertently tipped during flight.

In August, 1907, Lesh attempted, and accomplished, something completely new in world glider flying. He had his small craft attached to a 300-foot length of rope which was laid out straight along a cement dock. The opposite end was attached to a motorboat afloat on the St. Lawrence River. As Larry stood on the shore end, holding tightly to his glider, the boat moved off into midstream, gathering speed as it went. The line tightened and the young aeronaut sprinted full speed towards the end of the dock. A ten-mile wind was blowing off the water, and long before he had reached the river he had become airborne. Rising to a height of about fifty feet, his body dangling in space and supported by two wooden struts which passed under his armpits, he caused quite a stir along the Montreal waterfront.

As he clipped along at twenty miles an hour the glider was tossed about considerably by wind turbulences, but its teen-age pilot kept it under control by expert manipulation.

For seven miles downstream went the strange procession, until a spot opposite Pointe aux Trembles was reached, where Larry had planned to cast loose from the towrope and glide to shore.

He had told the occupants of the motorboat his intentions before the flight began, but in some way they had misunderstood. When they came opposite to the point they stopped the boat's engine, and Larry did not even have time to pull the cord which would have released the towrope.

The weight of the rope pulled the nose of the glider almost vertically down towards the water and the young pilot just had time to throw himself free before it plunged in. A good swimmer, Lesh was soon picked up and so was the glider, which suffered no damage except for its ducking.

In 1908 the clever young man built another glider to plans of his own, doing so in a rented workshop on St. Francis Xavier Street in Montreal.

During the first Aeronautical Society Meet, held at Morris Park, New York, the same year, he took his new glider there and, towed by an automobile, demonstrated his ability with a number of flights. At that meet he suffered the first accident of his flying career. The driver of the car put on too fast a burst of speed and the strain was just too much for the lightly-built glider. The wings folded back and Larry plunged down from a height of about twenty feet breaking a leg as he struck the ground with considerable force. With youth on his side, he quickly recovered. Shortly afterward his parents returned to again reside in the United States, and Montrealers were offered no further opportunities of seeing the young pilot in the air.

4. *Willard and the "Golden Flyer"*

WHEN CHARLES WILLARD made his first solo flight in the *Golden Flyer* he was a rank novice at the business of flying. His whole future in the air hinged on making good as Glenn Curtiss watched him from the ground. It was an anxious time for the daring young man.

The deafening uproar of the engine close behind him imparted strange feelings—scary, yes, but implying a power which helped greatly in bolstering his courage.

Perched on a precarious seat, right out in the open, just ahead of the lower wing and without a safety belt, the hurricane force of the wind beat against him as he gripped the controls with all the strength he possessed. As the machine lifted free from the ground he concentrated on everything Curtiss had told him. It would be unfair to say "taught him," because those two words simply do not fit.

Dual flying in the air with the *Golden Flyer* was impossible. The machine was the first one Glenn Curtiss ever built, and it had only one pilot seat. Even if it had possessed two, the meagre power of its small engine would not have lifted the weight of two men into the air.

The manner in which Curtiss taught the rudiments of flight control to his first pupil, was to run alongside the machine, grasping a wing tip strut, as Willard taxied up and down the field at a fast clip during preliminary training.

As Curtiss ran, he bellowed instructions to Willard at the top of his lungs. In later years Willard often joked at the mention of those first days. He recollected that with the howl of the engine in his ears, much of Curtiss' well-meant instructions were lost in the noise.

After three hours of that sort of thing there is little wonder that Curtiss decided to send Willard up on his first solo flight without further ado. Happily, Willard made a successful straight-away hop and landed without smashing a thing. Curtiss was fully satisfied, and the budding young pilot was launched on his flying career.

It all began in 1908 when a small group of Americans, interested in ballooning, had formed an offshoot of the Aero Club of America and titled themselves the Aeronautic Society, with the object of sponsoring airplane flights. They first endeavoured to bring from France a pilot named Delagrange, who owned a Farman biplane, hoping to stage the first public flying exhibition in the western hemisphere. Arrangements fell through and they looked around nearer home to see what could be done. After an interview with Glenn Curtiss, he offered to build them a plane for $5,000, the price also to include a pilot to fly it.

On July 17, 1909, the brand-new airplane was delivered to the Aeronautic Society, and it was the first craft to bear the name of Curtiss. Fragile in appearance, as were all of the pioneer aircraft, it was well designed and quite sturdily built. Its name, *Golden Flyer*, stemmed from the yellow colouring of the rubberized silk fabric used to cover the wing and control surfaces, together with the orange shellac which was used to paint the many wooden parts.

The front and rear control surfaces were attached to the wing framework by long bamboo spars, and a maze of piano wires led everywhere in order to brace the entire machine as a rigid whole. The ailerons for use in lateral control were attached to forward wing struts. .They were so large they actually slowed down the forward speed of the airplane to a marked degree, acting somewhat the same as landing flaps on modern aircraft although they were not supposed to do that.

Curtiss was a wizard at making engines. The motor in the *Golden Flyer* may seem a weakling today, but its four small cylinders could turn the propeller at 1,400 revolutions a minute, ample to get the airplane into the air and keep it flying at about fifty-five miles an hour.

Most flights in 1909 were not planned to last any length of time, yet it may sound almost unbelievable that the full capacity of the *Golden Flyer's* fuel tank was two gallons!

About the time the machine was nearing completion Charles Willard learned that its builder was on the lookout for a suitable fellow to fly it. Ambitious to get the job, he took the ferry to Long Island, New York, where Curtiss was making the craft in a shed at Mineola, and asked for the chance to make good. Curtiss liked his looks, and so Willard became the first pupil Curtiss ever trained.

Shortly after the arrival of the new plane and its novice pilot, the Aeronautic Society received its first request to fill a contract for a flying exhibition. It was rather a paradox that the machine, built to fly in the United States on its first exhibition, did nothing of the kind. The request for its use came from the management of the Scarboro Amusement Park, at Toronto, Ontario, and it was at once accepted. So Willard and the *Golden Flyer* trundled off to Canada by train, the plane contained in three huge packing cases.

When the young man reached the fair grounds, on August 28, 1909, he was in for a real shock. The committee which had arranged to have the machine flown at Toronto, had never even seen an airplane before, and they knew absolutely nothing of the requirements needed for takeoff and landing areas.

A very confined spot had been selected between some of the fair buildings, which covered only enough space on which to erect the tent in which the machine would be housed, and a tiny area in front where the craft could stand out in the open.

Willard took one look at the confined space and gasped, "What do they expect me to do, swoosh straight up out of the place like a sky rocket?"

However, he was a bright young man. After sizing things up, he decided he might make a getaway by using a straight run down an alley which separated two rows of concession stands. It was a mighty poor substitute for a runway. It led down to the waterfront and ended in a three-foot-drop breakwater lapped by Lake Ontario.

It was just as well Willard was an unperturbed amateur airman. If Curtiss had been there he would have taken one look at the whole layout and then have packed up and headed for home. The alleyway allowed only a six-foot clearance on either side of the wings, so to make sure the aircraft would follow a true course, Willard had a wooden trough made right down the centre. Into it he placed the front wheel of the machine's landing-gear and, presto, he had a straight and narrow track right down to the waterfront.

There was a lot of rain in the vicinity of Toronto in 1909— particularly that fall—and it was not until September 2nd that the airman was able to attempt his first flight. Dusk was fast drawing in under a lowering sky when he climbed aboard that day and, after a short engine run-up, he gave the signal to his helpers to let go.

With throttle wide open, the *Golden Flyer* moved down the makeshift "track," gaining speed with every foot. Then an unrealized factor entered the picture. The tire of the front wheel, rubbing against the sides of the trough, acted as a brake, and by the time the aircraft had reached the end of the runway its speed was not sufficient to make it airborne. It shot off into space all right from the top of the breakwater, but that was all it did do.

The flight had been billed as the grand finale for the day's activities at the exhibition, and although its ending was undoubtedly somewhat spectacular it was anything but grand. Wobbling along, it made a distance of about 300 feet out over the lake. Then it just could not keep up any longer. Down it went into the water with a mighty splash at a speed of about thirty miles an hour.

Willard later admitted his recollections of the affair were somewhat vague. The cold water took the breath clear out of him, and only the forward motion of the machine and the resultant rush of water against his body kept him tightly pressed in the seat. The craft had settled into about five feet of water, with the wheels resting on the bottom. It did not take long for Willard to be rescued and to have the *Golden Flyer* hauled out to dry land. Surprisingly it was quite undamaged, but the lower part and the engine was waterlogged.

It required five days to get it thoroughly dried out—particularly the engine—and on September 7th Willard was ready to try again. This time he used his head to good advantage, he had the inside of the wooden trough well lathered with soft soap! When he gave the *Flyer* the "gun" and whipped down the runway, it worked like a charm. As the craft shot off the end, out over the lake, it was fully airborne. Willard at last had the satisfaction of proving he could fly by making a circular flight well out over the lake, which carried him about five miles.

It had been his intention, when he returned, to land on a small strip of sandy beach near the breakwater, but when he came winging back he saw to his consternation that it was black with people. They had swarmed out from the fair grounds to the beach to watch his flight. Having just nowhere else to go, there was only a single choice for Willard, and a cold one at that. It meant another duck in the lake. So once again he plumped into it about thirty feet offshore.

It made a great splash but the airman was getting more or less used to it by this time, and he clung to the seat for all he was worth as the water flew in all directions. When the spray subsided he found himself sitting in the seat as before with the water just rippling around his neck. Salvage operations once more were in order. The aircraft was hauled back to its tent and the tiresome job of drying things out began all over again.

The oven of a nearby fish-and-chip stand was requisitioned for use in drying out the waterlogged magneto of the engine.

By September 11th, machine and motor seemed dried out enough for the daring young pilot to try yet another attempt. Late in the afternoon he tried his luck, and the *Golden Flyer* flashed down the runway and took to the air in perfect fashion. Willard had given strict instructions to the authorities to keep the beach clear of people so that he could land there when he came back. But this time he was beset with complications of a different nature.

The engine was running perfectly as he left the breakwater behind, when without warning it gave out a few coughs and quit. There was no chance of getting back to the beach, so once again into the water poor Willard plopped. After the plane had been pulled back to shore—shivering Willard with it—it was found that the propeller had been damaged in some manner, and the airman realized that the engine had stopped because of the magneto cutting out. Apparently the two previous immersions had proved too much fot it.

It was then that the disappointed pilot decided to call it a day, figuring he had done enough towards demonstrating an airplane in Canada. So he packed up, and returned to New York, and the first public flying exhibition in America came to a somewhat inglorious conclusion.

At the time of Willard's efforts at Toronto, the newspapers elsewhere in the world, as well as Toronto, were acclaiming the exploit of Admiral Robert E. Peary, who had just returned with the report that he had reached the North Pole. Little space was left in which to squeeze information about Willard's hard-won glory, and all the excitement he had caused at Scarboro Beach.

What small headlines there were about him, were most uncomplimentary. One read, "Willard goes up, Willard goes down," while another, less kindly, stated, "Willard prefers water to air."

He received no bouquets for the one excellent flight he did make. The fact that he had tested the cold waters of Lake Ontario three times in a row seemed to have cooled the reporters as much as it had chilled him.

Part two / MORE HISTORY MAKERS

5. *Charles Hamilton's*
"Aerial Clipper"

AFTER THE RECORDING in Part I of the first airplane flights in Nova Scotia and Ontario, some of the other Provinces where pioneer flying took place in Canada should not be overlooked.

Although the story of William Gibson of Victoria, B.C., and his two own-built airplanes has already been presented, it was given priority because he was one of Canada's own pioneers. But it must be stated that his activities in both British Columbia and in Alberta did not constitute flying "firsts" in either Province.

An American airman named Charles K. Hamilton earned the honour in British Columbia, and another American pilot, Hugh Robinson, was first to fly an airplane in Alberta.

Great excitement prevailed in the city of Vancouver when newspaper advertisements revealed that Hamilton and his own-built airplane would fly from an area on the outskirts of the city during the Easter weekend of 1910.

To accommodate the huge crowds expected to be on hand to witness the event, special street cars were put into service to carry them to and from Minoru Park racetrack, on Lulu Island, some miles out of the city where the flying was to take place.

A large tent was set up to house his airplane which arrived

29

well ahead of time, coming in three large crates from Seattle, where the airman had successfully concluded an exhibition flying contract.

With him when he reached Vancouver were his manager, Mr. H. C. Gretchell, and his mechanic, Charles Doley. Like numerous other airmen of that era who could afford it, Hamilton also had a private physician in attendance whenever he was in the air. It was a safety precaution which frequently paid off in the pioneer flying period, when an airman never knew from one flight to the next when the service of a qualified medical man might be needed in a hurry.

Good Friday was on April 25th, and on that date Hamilton made his first flight in Canada. A second one the same afternoon was also successful. Two flights of such a nature in a row brought considerable acclaim to the airman, and the thrilled spectators went home in wonderment in the realization that they had actually seen a man fly through the air on a flying machine.

Hamilton was back in the air on Saturday to make three individual flights, and a huge concourse of people were on hand to see him at his best. On one flight the daring pilot vanished from the sight of the throng as he flew upstream, following the Fraser River. He followed its course for twenty miles, to reach the city of New Westminster before he turned back. Excited citizens poured out into the streets as he flew over no higher than a hundred feet. Even the street cars stopped to allow people to alight for a better look, "as his queer-looking 'Aerial Clipper' sped past at the terrific speed of forty miles an hour," to quote one newspaper report.

The crowd at Lulu Island and his own personal friends became quite anxious as to his welfare, believing misfortune had overtaken him somewhere upstream. When they once again heard the roar of the engine as he returned, their relief was evident by the cheers that rose as Hamilton landed. He was accorded still greater acclaim when it was learned where he had been. No one there that day realized they had been on hand to witness the first "long" distance cross-country airplane flight to take place in Canada.

Hamilton was so numbed when he arrived back that he had to be assisted from the machine, and reports state that he was administered a stiff stimulating drink immediately he left the aircraft. Such measures would hardly meet with aircraft regulations today.

No flying was done on Easter Sunday, but on the Monday the airman was at it again, to total three flights during the afternoon in quite a boisterous wind. During one of them a unique contest was arranged, when a race was staged between the aircraft and a fast-running racehorse named Prince Brutus, ridden by jockey Curley Lewis.

The Minoru Park track distance was a mile in length and, realizing that his airplane was considerably faster than a galloping horse, Hamilton allowed his opponents a 660-yard start. It was a big handicap and it proved just a bit too much. The horse and rider won, but as they flashed past the winning post the airman was close behind and catching up fast.

During one of the other flights, Hamilton pocketed an apple before he took off and, later, as he was flying very low over the judges' stand, he dropped the apple. His aim was perfect and it hit the corner of the wooden stand, splattering the men inside with particles from head to foot. The "stunt" was announced as an effort to show how an airplane could be used in warfare to drop explosives, and apparently Hamilton made his point.

At the end of his last flight of the day, and also the final one he made in Vancouver, the airman went up to about five hundred feet, and when directly above the infield he stopped the motor and put the plane into a vertical dive for the field. He held it until everyone believed he was about to crash, then suddenly he pulled the craft back to a glide and landed on the infield without once making use of his engine. It was a real climax to his flying, but dangerous stuff, and many pilots of that risky flying era lost their lives trying to do the selfsame thing. It did prove, however, that Hamilton had little regard for his own neck.

6. Ely Battles the Prairie Winds

ALMOST THREE MONTHS after Hamilton's appearance in Vancouver in 1910 another American airman, named Eugene Ely, shipped his machine up from the United States to Manitoba at the invitation of the exhibition committee of the City of Winnipeg. He was not as successful in his flying efforts as Hamilton had been, but it was not because he lacked nerve or did not possess a flyable airplane.

The boisterous prairie wind proved to be a tough adversary against him all the time he was at the Manitoba capital in July, 1910.

When he did not get into the air as advertised on the 14th, spectators at the fair ground openly expressed their opinions that he was a fake. Few cared a single jot that the pilot might be risking his neck to attempt to fly in such strong winds. It is doubtful if people then realized that the forty-mile wind that was blowing was about the same speed as the full forward motion of Ely's plane in calm air. If he had gone up on the 14th he could have hardly made any headway into such a wind. More probably, it would have been blown backwards and wrecked. Things did not turn out much better in any event in the end.

On the 15th the wind was still howling across Winnipeg from out of the western prairie, but the jibes he had received drove

32

the airman to fly against his better judgment. Fortunately, his initial Canadian battle against the elements was quite successful, although his machine pitched and rocked about in flight as though it was a crazy thing. The flight lasted only a few minutes and the people were far from satisfied, and said so in a most uncomplimentary fashion.

Feeling that he had to vindicate himself, in spite of the risk he knew prevailed, he climbed into the seat and set off once again to try to pacify the spectators. He treated them to another few minutes' flight, as rough for him as the other had been, but when he tried to make a landing all his skill proved to no avail.

A gust of wind blasted his craft just as the wheels touched down on the infield of the exhibition racetrack, and one wing was lifted high in the air as the other smashed into the ground. Then the landing-gear collapsed and was ripped away, and seconds later the fragile biplane was a pathetic wreck. As the cloud of dust drifted away on the wind, Ely was seen to step from the jumbled heap and, remarkably enough, he was quite uninjured.

Ely never flew in Canada again—and no wonder—but even so, his brief visit and efforts made flying history, because his short flights were the first ever to be made at any point on the Canadian prairies.

The people of Winnipeg perhaps felt better towards him later in the year. When he flew there in July, 1910, his feet were only on the lower rungs of the ladder of fame but on November 14, 1910, he received world-wide acclaim. On that date he became the first airman to fly an airplane off the deck of a battleship, doing so from the U.S.S. *Birmingham*, which was anchored at Hampton Roads, Virginia.

So whether they knew it or not, Winnipegonians did see a clever airman in action that long ago day, regardless of their first impressions.

7. The "Red Devil" Visits Saint John

THIS IS NOT an account of a Biblical legend involving a meeting of the Devil with Saint John, although the title may imply such an affair. Yet such a meeting did take place as history reveals, and it happened in Canada a long time ago.

As related in the first pages of this book, Canada's own John McCurdy was the first pilot to fly anywhere in the eastern Maritime Provinces, but as his flying took place on Cape Breton Island there still remains the story of who was the first to make a flight from the mainland of the maritimes.

This event, and the first time an airplane ever flew in New Brunswick, fell to the lot of an American airman in 1912.

At that time a famous inventor, named Captain Thomas Baldwin, from south of the border, had designed and built a very successful airplane to which he gave the somewhat startling name of the *Red Devil*. It was a massive affair compared with most of the airplanes of that date, weighing 1,050 pounds—over half a ton—and that without the pilot. Fortunately it had an equally sturdy engine to power it, one which developed 80 h.p.— enough to enable the machine to fly quite well.

The Saint John's exhibition committee arranged with Baldwin to have his big aircraft shipped up to Canada from New York to play a part in their annual exhibition, held every August, and as Baldwin was unable to come with the machine himself he hired a pilot to fly the craft in his stead.

34

His choice was good when he sent along a clever young airman named Cecil Peoli, already quite distinguished in the United States in the art of flying.

On the last day of August, 1912, several huge packing cases arrived at Saint John, and inside them was the disassembled parts of the *Red Devil*. Peoli took just one look at the exhibition grounds from which he was supposed to fly and saw at once it was far too small from which to operate.

Casting about for a better site, he finally decided to make use of the foreshore of the Courtenay Bay flats, which was ideal at low tide and was on the outskirts of town, near Redwood Park. There he set about rigging the big machine, and September 2nd saw him in the air for the first time.

As takeoffs and landings could only be made during low tides, when the beach was available, the advertised schedules of the times he was supposed to fly went very much awry. However, until the 6th he managed to get into the air for several flights each day, and being a conscientious fellow, on every occasion he flew low over the exhibition grounds so the people there could enjoy the spectacle of seeing an airplane in flight.

On one trip he flew so low he struck a number of poles on which flags were flying, but fortunately his machine was not damaged, and he flew merrily on his way.

The real highlight of his visit to Saint John came for one of the city's residents on September 5. That day New Brunswick chalked up its first aerial passenger flight when a local citizen, Mr. Horace Porter, was carried aloft on a flight which lasted eleven minutes. He sat on an improvised perch directly behind the pilot, which in a way was a nice thing to do, because the spot was fairly well sheltered from the driving blast of the wind in flight.

Mr. Porter was one of the directors of the fair, and it was an exhilarating experience for him to look down from the air at the whole spread of the exhibition, whose destinies he had helped to guide for many years.

At the end of the flight, Peoli made an excellent landing on the hard-packed sands of the tidewater flats, and after he and his passenger had alighted he turned to Mr. Porter and asked, "Well, how'd you like it?"

Mr. Porter replied, "The flight was wonderful, but I sure didn't like that steep dive you made, just before you accomplished the landing."

It was then that the exhibition director received a real shock. Peoli was silent a moment or two and then, as a wan smile formed on his lips, he said, "You know, Mr. Porter, I didn't dive intentionally, it was your added weight in front of the machine that caused it to dip so steeply."

The airman then confided to the astonished Mr. Porter that a front control elevator had been removed after the first day, as it was not needed with one person aboard, and taking it off lessened head resistance. As a consequence, when Peoli nosed down to make a landing the craft was very sluggish in straightening out as he pulled back on the controls to flatten out for a good landing.

The *Red Devil* had almost become unmanageable at a lower landing speed, and the swift dive towards the earth nearly ended in tragedy.

No more passengers were taken up after that until the flying closed with the exhibition on September 6th, and Mr. Porter thanked his lucky stars for his narrow escape from death, while Peoli went off to seek further laurels.

8. *Two Brave-Hearted Women*

TODAY WOMEN FORM a large quota of passengers who travel by air, but how few of them know that the first Canadian women to fly as passengers in Canada did so as far back as the year of 1912?

The first one was Mrs. Olive Stark.

How would you like to take an aerial ride, sitting on a precarious improvised seat made from a length of wooden board, roughly attached to the top of a wing? There would not be many takers for a ride like that today.

We must not overlook the fact that the "seat" was right out in the open, with the passenger's legs dangling in space, with nothing beneath except the ground far below.

It is a spine-tingling thought, yet that is exactly how Mrs. Stark became the first woman to fly in an airplane in the Dominion, and a rough exciting business it was, as she sped through the air at a sixty-mile-an-hour clip. The strong wind buffeted her unmercifully, trying its best to dislodge her, but she held on like grim death, for to let go would have meant just that.

Perhaps she would not have been quite so willing to take the risk with any airman but the pilot who persuaded her to go aloft was her own husband, who was well qualified for the job.

Both Billy Stark and his wife were Canadian born, but he had learned to fly at the Curtiss Flying School, North Island, near San Diego, in 1912, and had returned to Vancouver with a newly-purchased brand new Curtiss pusher biplane.

37

After he had established flying quarters at Minoru Park racetrack, a few miles south of the port city, he began his exploits as a Canadian exhibition pilot and earned for himself considerable fame in British Columbia.

Mrs. Stark's flight took place from the Minoru Racetrack, on April 24, 1912. As the airplane was designed to carry only the pilot, taking Mrs. Stark up presented quite a problem, but it was overcome simply by making a place for her to sit. The machine was wide open to the wind and the only feasible spot to attach the length of board was on the upper part of the lower wing, just to the left of the pilot's seat.

Mrs. Stark was wearing her ordinary outdoor clothing at the time, which included a long flowing dress, which certainly was not suitable apparel for sitting on a wing in mid-air. Quite a bit of difficulty was experienced in installing her on the seat, and a wooden box had to be fetched from the track's storeroom to enable her to climb up to get aboard. The seat had no back of course, and she soon learned it was a most uncomfortable prospect she had before her, as the sharp edge of the plank pressed against her legs. Nothing daunted, she hung on tightly to the wires which crossed in front of her as Billy's helpers started up the engine and the propeller bit into the air.

Olive possessed no safety belt of any kind, nor was she fastened to the machine in any way. All that prevented her from being blown off into space when in full flight was her own ability to hang on. Insurance salesmen today would take a dim view of such a caper, and for that matter maybe they would have done the same in 1912. Mrs. Stark's prospects of a long life did not appear too rosy to the little knot of spectators who watched as Billy gave the engine the "gun" and the craft shot down the infield and into the air.

In keeping with the times, Olive wore an immense "flying hat," a huge woollen contraption, supposedly made for the job of keeping one warm and the hair from becoming unruly. As the aircraft circled above the field at an altitude of 300 feet, the wind finally got the best of the "bonnet" and whipped it off Olive's head without warning.

As she was sitting only a few feet ahead of the pusher propeller, the headgear was swept into the revolving blades and, catching on one, was whirled round and round at high speed. Off balance with the added weight, the propeller set up a tremendous vibration throughout the entire machine, shaking it in such an alarming manner Billy thought that any moment the craft would fall apart, and the two of them would be dashed to earth and killed.

After a few minutes of this hair-raising experience, the hat fell free, the vibration suddenly stopped, and the two aboard thankfully realized that danger was past.

While the flight was in progress, the bulky skirt worn by Olive flapped and banged around her legs in an alarming manner, and at times her limbs were forcibly thrust backwards under the wing, causing aches and pains for several days after the flight had successfully ended.

After returning to the racetrack Mrs. Stark had to be lifted from the wing, as the strain of hanging on had almost exhausted her. However, there was no fear in her eyes when she was asked how she had weathered the experience, and she stated she would willingly do it again any time, providing her husband was the pilot.

Although Mrs. Stark's flight might easily be classed as a rather suicidal affair, nevertheless it was a most courageous undertaking and fortunately the account of it has not been lost to history.

The second daring young woman to became an airplane passenger in Canada was Miss Dora Labatt of London, Ontario.

Coincidentally, her experience also took place in 1912, so eastern Canada shares with the west in having recorded the flight of a woman at such an early date in air history.

Miss Labatt's trip came as a complete surprise to her, but when the opportunity presented she accepted the challenge without a moment's hesitation.

Hers was every bit as exciting as the one experienced by Olive Stark, but it was somewhat more comfortable. She did not have to perch on a rickety seat, roughly attached to a wing, because the craft she went up in was blessed with two seats, one for the pilot and one for a passenger, although like Stark's Curtiss both were right out in the open and the plane's occupants were equally subject to the full blast of the wind in flight.

The summer holiday resort of Port Stanley, on Lake Erie, was celebrating the opening of an electric railway connecting the lakeside holiday spot with the town of London, Ontario. To add an additional drawing card to the affair the festival committee decided to have an airplane on hand to make exhibition flights, and their choice of an airman was good.

They contacted an American pilot named Walter Brookins, already established as one of the best fliers in the country, who had many flying records to his credit, including a world altitude record of over a mile in height. By train he brought along to Port Stanley a type of airplane never previously seen in flight in Canada. The craft was a two-seater (side by side) Burgess-Wright seaplane, which at that period of aviation vocabulary was termed a hydroplane.

During the first three days of his flying at Port Stanley, which commenced on July 17, 1912, Brookins did not carry any passengers. The big event for Miss Labatt and spectators alike took place on the 20th.

Officials extended the opportunity of a flight to her because she was one of the most popular of London's younger set and, when the question was put to her, "Would you like to have a ride?" she excitedly agreed, although it was a dark and raincast day. It was quite obvious that the prospect of a really pleasant flight could be ruled out but it did not faze her, and on approaching the craft as it was drawn up on the beach, she expressed the opinion that it looked like a strange sea animal awaiting to gobble her up. So, appropriately, she named it "The Beast."

The two seats the machine possessed were ranged alongside each other in front of the lower wing, clamped down to a fragile-looking yet solid framework. The word "seats" may lead one to envision comfortable padded affairs for flying enjoyment, but such was far from the case. Actually, they were narrow uncomfortable things, with stiff wooden backs. Each had a small belt as a safety aid, and that was real progress in a flying era when most airmen scoffed at such things.

Prepared for her flight, Miss Labatt also wore a large-sized headgear, much in use about that time for riding in open automobiles. It was kept on by means of a chiffon scarf wrapped tightly around it and then tied firmly under the chin of the wearer.

Once she was stowed aboard, Brookins climbed into his seat, the engine began to roar, and they were off. The lake was quite choppy with a brisk off-the-water wind, and Miss Labatt received quite a bouncing before the seaplane rose smoothly into the air. Although the flight was of short duration there was no other girl in the whole of Canada that day who was more thrilled than Miss Labatt. When the flight came to an end and she was lifted from her seat and carried through shallow water at the beach, miraculously enough her big chapeau was still firmly on her head.

A large crowd of spectators lining the shore gave her a rousing ovation as she walked up the beach, but few if any then realized they had witnessed a bright spot in Canadian air history on that otherwise gloomy afternoon.

9. Daring Alys, and Tiny Eileen

ALMOST EVERY NEWSPAPER we read today reveals some activity connected with aviation in which women are involved. Such information, however, holds no hint of the astonishing fact that women earned a place in air history a long long time ago. The exploits of some date back to the early pioneer era, at the time when men were only just beginning to learn to fly.

The first flight by a woman pilot does not go quite that far back in Canada's air history, but it does belong in the year before the outbreak of World War One. The name of the daring woman was Alys McKey Bryant, and to her alone goes the glory. She died in Washington, D.C., in 1954.

American born and raised, she learned to fly in California in 1912, doing so in an exceedingly hazardous and haphazard fashion. She first became interested in the idea of becoming a pilot when she spotted an advertisement in a Los Angeles newspaper in the summer of 1912.

The advertisement stated that a woman pupil was required to be taught to fly, and that the successful applicant would receive full training without cost, providing she would later be willing to become an "exhibition pilot" with the Bryant Brothers Air Show. Out of a number of applicants, Alys was chosen because she had ridden a motorcycle several times, a feat which apparently impressed Mr. Bennett, the Bryants' manager.

In spite of the exciting advertisement Alys' first introduction to aviation was not as a flying pupil. The aircraft the Bryants owned had been smashed up badly the week she got the job, and so she had to pitch in to help repair it, before any tuition could begin. The three brothers, John, Henry and Frank, lived at Palm Springs, and their flying field was right alongside their ranch home.

Because of several flying contracts at various California points where the aircraft had to be utilized, Alys' air training progressed very slowly. When it did begin it was particularly difficult for her because the biplane was only a single-seater. All of the instruction she received before she actually went solo was by verbal method from John, together with many taxiing runs up and down the flying field.

It is not surprising, therefore, that she did not make her first solo flight until December, 1912, but she had learned well and, as she was an apt pupil, it was a complete success.

Contracts to fly during 1913 had been negotiated by manager Bennett with several cities and smaller places in the northwest states. Also at Vancouver and Victoria in British Columbia. Because of this, operational headquarters were moved from Palm Springs to Seattle in February, 1913.

With makeshift quarters established on reclaimed land known as Harbour Island, Alys received final training. She had to make good. It was necessary for her to prove to the Tillicum Club of Seattle that she was fully qualified to handle the airplane in the air before final contract negotiations could be signed.

The Tillicums were sponsoring the Bryants' flying. During 1912 they had been badly let down by another airman, whose promise to produce a lady pilot did not materialize. Having no wish for a repetition of such a fiasco in 1913 they made sure plans would not again go astray. Both Johnny and Alys made qualifying flights of short duration on April 8th, to the Club's full approval, and the contract was signed to everyone's satisfaction.

To prove just how clever she was, Alys made her first exhibition flight over Seattle a few days later, going over the centre of the city at a height of 2,000 feet. It took real courage to do a thing like that. As Alys looked at her instruments, checking flight time and height, she could have been excused if the sight of them caused some consternation. All the machine possessed was a second-hand altimeter fastened to the control column with electric tape and a dollar watch fastened to her knee with a length of cord!

The Bennett Flyers, as the group had now named themselves, felt that they were well on the way to further glories. With contracts waiting them at the Portland Rose Festival and a fair at Yakima, things looked quite rosy.

Alys' flying at Seattle was in connection with the Golden Potlatch festivities, held annually to commemorate the first arrival of gold shipments to that port from the Yukon. Because of the excellent flying she accomplished, she was named the Golden Potlatch Girl for 1913, and no woman before or since deserved the title more.

By this time Cupid had been busy. He had shot a couple of arrows straight and true to the hearts of Alys and Johnny, and their love blossomed quickly to a marriage at Seattle in May.

The contract to fly in Canada, at Vancouver, B.C., was scheduled to start on July 31st. They were on the job and ready to go, right on the dot, doing so from the old Minoru Park racetrack situated on Lulu Island, not far from the city.

Johnny took the biplane up for the first short flight as a test. Shortly after he had landed, brave Alys was installed in the single seat and away she went. Before the astounded eyes of several thousand spectators, she circled high above, making figures of eights and a number of "dips" before she returned to the grounds to receive a tremendous ovation from admiring fans.

Unlike many famous firsts which were accomplished without people realizing they were seeing history made, it was known that Alys' flight was the first to be made by a woman pilot in Canada. The crowd was primed for the occasion and came up with a tremendous reception for the courageous girl as she stepped down from the machine.

Both Johnny and Alys made several more flights before the "meet" was completed on August 1st. They then dismantled their machine and sent it aboard a ship to Victoria, where they were billed to make their next exhibition on the 5th.

Alys was the first Bryant to fly at Victoria. After taking off from the Willows racetrack, she had planned to fly over the downtown area of the city and to circle above the Parliament Buildings. Nature quickly took a hand in changing her intentions. A boisterous westerly was blowing straight from the Pacific Ocean, and the airplane was buffeted about like a feather on the wind. The airwoman could scarcely make headway against it. After sixteen minutes in the air she gave up trying and quickly came winging back to the racetrack where she made a safe but bumpy landing.

When interviewed by reporters shortly after her return, she said, "I don't want a ride like that again. It was the roughest, toughest and most fearsome flight I have so far experienced." She was a courageous girl even to have tried it and, as circumstances developed, it was to be the last she ever made.

The following day Johnny was flying over the centre of Victoria at about 800 feet when his machine went into a dive. No one of course knows what happened up there, but the dive grew steeper and steeper with every second. As the spectators in the streets below watched aghast they saw the wings fold back and in a twinkling the aircraft was a mass of wreckage in the air. Seconds later it had plunged from sight, to crash on the roof of the Lee Dye Building in the heart of Victoria's Chinatown. Help was quickly forthcoming, but Johnny was beyond all need of human aid.

Though he died that day, his name still lives in Canada's flying history, for he was the first airman to meet death in the Dominion because of a flying accident. When destiny stepped in that fateful summer day, which now seems so long ago, depriving Alys of her two great loves, Johnny and flying, it wrote finish to her active career in the air and she never piloted an airplane again.

It would be remiss to describe the flying exploits of Alys Bryant without also mentioning the achievement of the first Canadian girl to become a pilot. In this case there was no huge throng of spectators on hand to watch or to offer her acclaim when she landed. Her first solo flight caused no excitement of any kind except in the heart of Eileen Vollick, the brave young woman involved. Fortunately, the facts relating to her can be kept fresh, saving them from the oblivion they might easily have received.

Perhaps the flying done by women in other countries urged Miss Vollick to learn what she could do. Whatever was the cause, she applied to the Elliot Air Service Flying School in her home city of Hamilton, Ontario, requesting enrolment as a student. Officials of the company were at first openly dubious whether she would be able to handle an airplane in flight. To be quite fair to them, there was good reason for their belief. Eileen was not an Amazon type, she stood only five feet one inch in height, and weighed but 89 pounds. Diminutive though she was, her determination to become a pilot was intense. Her firmness outweighed all company objections, and she was finally enrolled at the beginning of the winter of 1927.

The doubting instructors quickly changed their minds about her ability, soon realizing they had a born pilot as their first lady pupil. She was so tiny, two seat cushions had to be placed in the pilot seat she occupied to enable her to see above the sides of the cockpit.

All of the flying instruction she received took place during the winter months, a very unpleasant time of the year to do so, in an open-cockpit Curtiss "Jenny" biplane. Temperatures most of the time stood well below freezing, and on a number of occasions when she was aloft it was below zero.

The frozen surface of Lake Ontario was utilized as a "flying field," the aircraft being fitted with ski undergear for the purpose. History records Miss Vollick as being the first woman on the North American continent to pilot a ski-equipped airplane, and undoubtedly anywhere in the world.

A clever pupil, she quickly mastered the art of flight, making her first solo flight in February and her final tests on March 13, 1928. At the time her full flying time was sixteen hours. Under the very watchful eyes of a Canadian government air inspector, she passed all her tests like a veteran and was granted private pilot's licence number 77.

What later became of Canada's first woman pilot has been lost in the mists of time. She did stay with flying for a year or so after becoming a pilot, but her marriage seems to have brought an end to that career. She left Hamilton to reside in New York in the early nineteen-thirties, and there among the millions of people she was swallowed up so far as Canadian air history is concerned. In all probability she gave up flying entirely to concentrate on her home life, relinquishing her flying ambitions, which if she had continued might well have brought her into national prominence as Canada's premier airwoman.

Part
three / FAR HORIZONS

10. Many Records Fell
to "Jenny"

THE CURTISS JN4 two-seater biplane, which was used exclusively to train airmen in Canada during World War One, had an engine of only 90 h.p.   Seventy-five miles an hour was just about its top speed in flight, but what it lacked in that ability was somewhat balanced by the craft's sturdy construction.   It was one airplane that could really take a beating, both in the air and on the ground.

The JN4 was early nicknamed "Jenny," the word having been coined from the manufacturer's registration letters, JN. Thousands of pilots, and others connected with the destiny of those airplanes, used the term quite endearingly when referring to JN's during the war and in later peacetime use.

A great many JN4's were in use at the various aerodromes established in eastern Canada in 1917 and 1918, under Royal Flying Corps and later under Royal Air Force jurisdiction.   It was during the latter year that a "Jenny" of military status was used on an undertaking far removed from a military operation, yet one which made flying history in Canada.

During 1918, recruiting for prospective pilots for military service began to show a marked decrease in some parts of Canada, and Montreal was one of the larger centres where it was felt something should be done to arouse lagging interest.

In an effort to stir things up, Captain Brian A. Peck of the 89th Training Squadron at Leaside, North Toronto, was commissioned to fly to Montreal and was supplied with suitable leaflets to be dropped over the heart of the city, as he demonstrated a few aerial aerobatics above.

Accompanying him on the trip was Corporal Mathers as engineer, and plans went well until they reached Montreal when wet weather engulfed them for three days, and flying over the city had to be cancelled. After waiting it out, Air Force Headquarters instructed him to fly back to Toronto and let the recruiting mission slide. Before he set off on the return trip, Peck was approached by several Montreal businessmen, who suggested he carry back to Toronto a bag of mail to inaugurate air-mail flying in Canada. The airman thought the idea a splendid one and, contacting headquarters, he was given authority to carry out the plan.

Mail was prepared for the trip by being officially cancelled at the Montreal Post Office, and upon each envelope to be flown the imprint of a rubber stamp read, "Inaugural Service, via Aerial Mail, Montreal, 23.6.18." June 23rd turned out to be just as rainy as the few previous days, so takeoff for Toronto was postponed until the 24th when the weather cleared a little. Even so, it was not a good day for flying, as fast-scudding rain clouds were hurrying past from the west at a height of less than five hundred feet.

Peck used the Polo Field at Dominion Park, near Montreal, for his operations, and when he and Mathers set off on the 24th they had great difficulty in getting out of the place as the engine was not developing full power because of poor gasoline with which they had been obliged to fill up the tank at Montreal.

In any case they had to stay below the clouds to keep in visual touch with the ground, as it was their only means of finding their way out of the city. Flying at fifty feet above the mainline railway track, they were doing nicely when out of the mist ahead loomed the high structure of a bridge. Only just in the nick of time was it spotted by Peck who banked away, missing the massive structure by inches.

By the time they had reached Kingston the spark plugs were beginning to foul up from the low-grade fuel used, and the engine was coughing and spluttering alarmingly. Landing there, Mathers cleaned them up and once again they went on their way, stopping first at Camp Deseronto, an R.A.F. aerodrome on the northeastern shore of Lake Ontario. Then off they went again to complete their flight at Toronto. After arrival, Peck immediately boarded an army motor vehicle and was whisked down to Toronto's main post-office, where he delivered into the postmaster's own hands the 120 letters he had flown from Montreal. As the first official air-mail ever flown in Canada, each of the envelopes are today valued at $250 per specimen.

When World War One ended the Canadian government disposed of its surplus training airplanes and a huge stock of parts to a Toronto firm, who in turn offered them for sale. Prices of individual airplanes varied from $1,200 to $3,500, depending on the condition they were in.

During 1919, and until the end of 1920, no government supervision of civil airplanes or pilots was in effect. The absence of such control allowed dozens of ex-war pilots, and some civilians, to fly either for themselves or as pilots with newly-formed flying companies which sprang into being in widely separated points in Canada. Not all of the pilots were competent or as careful as could have been desired. As a consequence, wrecked JN4 aircraft soon began to dot the Canadian landscape from coast to coast.

Fortunately for flying in Canada, there were also many who did not possess the reckless spirit and devil-may-care attitude. It was the saner ones who established civil flying in the Dominion on a solid footing, and traditions and flying records of an outstanding nature resulted.

Several branches of the Aerial League of the British Empire were formed—one at Montreal becoming quite active—while two others in western Canada, situated at Victoria and Vancouver, were the most progressive of all. By early spring of 1919, the latter two had purchased four "Jennies" each, and flying activities began early in May.

To show what they could do, pilots Alfred Eckley and Ernest Hall paid a friendly visit by air to Victoria, flying across the wide stretch of the Gulf of Georgia on May 13, 1919. When they flew back to Vancouver the following day they had established a record, being the first airmen to negotiate the over-water flight between the Canadian mainland and Vancouver Island.

Not to be outdone, the Victoria members cooked up a trip of their own, and on May 18th pilots Robert Rideout and Harry Brown set off in a JN4, named the *Pathfinder*, their destination the United States city of Seattle. A single letter they carried was addressed to the Mayor of Seattle. What became of it or its envelope is unknown, but it was the first piece of aerial mail flown between the two cities. When the airmen flew back to Victoria on May 19th, a number of letters went with them. The few specimens which have survived are today worth $75 each.

One flight almost cost the life of one of the members of the Victoria branch, and through no fault of his own. Harry Brown, in 1920, was heading northward, with the intention of giving the people who lived at Prince Rupert their first thrill of flying. He was flying alone in a "Jenny" which had had its wheel undergear replaced by pontoons, to convert the craft into a seaplane, and better fitted for over-water flights. All went well until after the airman had left Alert Bay on the west coast on what should have been the last hop to Prince Rupert. When he was miles off shore, over open water, the engine suddenly quit. A heavy swell was running on the sea below, but he had no choice except to go down and, fortunately, he was able to effect a good landing.

His examination of the motor proved the magneto was not functioning, and as he could not make repairs, when darkness came he made himself as snug as possible in the open cockpit, with the intention of sitting it out through the night.

Then the wind began to freshen and, with the set of the tide, the airplane was carried onto the rocks off Nalan Island. The high waves soon began to break the fragile "Jenny" to pieces, so the airman took to the water, and only after exhaustive efforts was he able to reach shore through the pounding surf.

Daylight revealed no sign of the stricken JN4. The ocean had completely swallowed it up, and Brown was alone on the island without equipment of any kind. Cold, wet and hungry, he was in a truly tight spot, marooned off a barren coast and completely without drinking water, food or shelter, and the few matches he had in his pocket were a pulp.

Knowing his location was miles off the regular north-and-southbound coastwise shipping route, the airman realized it was up to himself to effect his own survival. The fortitude which had earned for him the Military Cross in the air during World War One was still a primary part of his make-up, so he set about planning a means of escape.

The shore was strewn with drift logs so, selecting one suited to his purpose, together with a flat length of driftwood, he straddled his makeshift boat and pushed off to sea. He planned to paddle over the still turbulent water to reach the shipping lanes, far to the west.

Twenty-three wet and weary hours later, he was spotted by the sharp eyes of a lookout from the deck of the United States ship, *Hidden Inlet*, southbound from Alaska for Seattle. Brown was played out when picked up, far out on the open water of Queen Charlotte Sound and about twenty miles southwest of Bella Bella and the mainland coast.

The greatest single exploit accomplished by the Vancouver branch of the Aerial League made top air history when one of its pilots set off eastward and conquered the vast barrier of the Rocky Mountains by air for the first time. Plans for the attempt originated in July, 1919, and the route selected for the aerial crossing of the continental divide was by way of the Crawford Pass, to Lethbridge, then north to Calgary.

None of the Curtiss biplanes the club possessed was over-burdened with power. The ninety horse-power engine with which each of their "Jennies" were fitted could barely lift a machine to altitudes higher than seven thousand feet.

To select the Vancouver airman for the flight attempt lots were drawn. There could only be one occupant of the two-seater, because the spare cockpit was to hold an additional fuel tank to ensure lengthier flying time should it be needed on some of the laps along the way.

Result of the draw proved pilot Ernest Hoy to be the fortunate winner, and on August 7, 1919, he squeezed his bulky frame into the rear cockpit, roared down the infield of the Minoru Park racetrack, and air history was in the making. A small bag of officially cancelled letters also went along in the crowded cockpit.

The route planned to Lethbridge followed a zigzag course, going by way of some of the great mountain valleys with stops for refuelling at Vernon, Grand Forks and Cranbrook.

Unseen air currents and vicious down-drafts plagued Hoy all the way. Frequently the heavily-loaded craft was barely able to scrape over the heights of land connecting one valley to another, and sometimes only a few feet separated the wheels of the labouring plane from the treetops beneath.

Arriving at Lethbridge, the airman did not stay long. Quickly refuelling, he was off on the last lap for Calgary. Night had almost settled down by the time he arrived at the Foothill City, but the switched-on lights from hundreds of cars, whose owners were on hand to see him arrive, aided Hoy in a good landing on open prairie at Bowness Park, west of the city. The entire flight from Vancouver to Calgary was accomplished during the one day, and was made in an elapsed time of sixteen hours and forty minutes, during twelve hours and fifteen minutes of which Hoy was in the air.

The letters he carried were soon snapped up by collectors who purchased them from the original recipients; and today each envelope of that mail is valued at $275.

It would be well to pause a moment to consider the difference in Hoy's flight and the manner in which it is done today.

From the great height at which modern air liners now go over, the mountains appear as mere nothings, just mounds of green and brown with cream-puff tops. Not to Hoy did they look like that. To him they were a tremendous menace, their lofty peaks spearing the sky at altitudes he could never hope to reach. He had none of the warmth of a closed cabin nor man-made landing fields. He just did it the hard way, blazing the air trail along which so many were later to follow.

It is a long time since his epic journey took place, but Canadians can still look back at the exploit with pride and say of pilot Ernest Hoy, "Thanks a lot, for a job well done."

Another adventure in which a "Jenny" played a major role in Canada also involved the author of this book. The affair still holds vivid memories for me, so I can do no better than recount the experience in the first person.

It took place when I "jumped" into flying history by making a parachute descent at Crystal Beach, Ontario, on July 5, 1919.

One thing I shall never forget was the sudden tightening of the muscles of my tummy that July day, as I clambered out of the "Jenny's" rear cockpit and looked down into the void below, as I stood on the wing. I was poised on the threshold of my first parachute jump, which turned out to be the first one to be made by a Canadian from an airplane flying in Canada. Believe me, at that moment I would have been happy to trade places with anyone in the world, to have been in their shoes and they in mine. Unfortunately for them, if such had taken place, they would have found themselves perched on the wing as bare-footed as Tom Sawyer ever was. The only things I wore as I stood, hanging on to the fuselage against the wind, was the parachute body harness, a partially inflated inner tube and a bathing suit.

I was not scared, but it was a tense situation all right. I had become a pilot before the outbreak of World War One, when I had taught myself to fly in a Curtiss pusher biplane that my partner, Tom Blakely, and I had built at Calgary, Alberta. Even during later service in the Royal Flying Corps and the Royal Air Force, the thought of voluntarily parachuting from an airplane in full flight had never previously entered my head. Then suddenly, there I was standing on a wing, two thousand feet above Lake Erie, with only a moment to go before I plunged into space.

Even on July 4, 1919, I would have bet a million dollars—figuratively, of course —that I would never bail out of an airplane in mid-air, yet by the evening of the very next day I had done so. No one can ever convince me that destiny does not work in devious ways.

After being demobilized from war service in May, 1919, an ex-war pilot friend, Don Russell, offered me a job as airplane mechanic, connected with a civil flying organization. Jobs were not plentiful at that time, and to have the opportunity of staying with flying seemed heaven-sent. I snapped at the chance.

Russell's relatives had furnished the money to finance a flying company, which they named Allied Aeroplanes, Ltd., of Brantford, Ontario. A couple of two-seater Curtiss JN4 aircraft had already been purchased from war-surplus stocks, and the firm needed only an engineer to complete the picture. They had big plans for making money, carrying passengers aloft on ten-minute flights at ten dollars a ride.

Crystal Beach, at the eastern end of Lake Erie, on the Canadian side, offered good prospects so we were despatched there to set up shop. Most of the residents of the resort's summer homes and practically all the daily visitors to the place were Americans, hailing from Buffalo, N.Y., across the lake, and from other points farther afield. Huge crowds poured into the resort, especially at week-ends, being ferried over from Buffalo on two large ferries which plied back and forth seven days a week.

As news of our flying activities began to get around business boomed, and on July 3rd our manager, Neil Macmillan, received a phone call from Buffalo. It came from the Irvin Parachute Company, a small firm at that date, who were involved in the development and making of aerial life preservers. They inquired if one of Allied Aeroplanes' "Jennies" could be utilized from which to test a new type of parachute they had designed.

Macmillan at once consented, and early on the morning of July 4th Mr. Leslie Irvin arrived at our tent headquarters at Crystal Beach. Accompanying him was a Mr. Chilson, and between them they carried a bulky bundle. They revealed it contained their newest development, a back-pack type of parachute of a more advanced design than any previously used.

Compared with the compact equipment worn by airmen today it was a cumbersome looking affair. It appeared and weighed more like a bag of cement than an aerial life preserver. No airmen today would willingly wear such a monstrosity in a modern aircraft. In fact, the seating space of most airplanes today would preclude all possibility of its use.

Just the same it was a famous bundle of flying history, because it was the granddaddy of all such back-pack types of parachutes in use today. Too, it is worth recording that a vast number of lives have been saved in emergencies in the air, all over the world, by the use of chutes which were sired by that original Irvin ancestor.

To wear the apparatus, it was fastened to the jumper's back, being firmly held in place by three buckled straps. One fitted neatly around the chest, the other two being adjusted just as snugly around either thigh. Fastened on as tightly as they were, there was no possibility of accidently slipping out of the harness, but—one disadvantage it held—neither could it be released in a hurry.

Chilson had come over from Buffalo specially to test the chute, and as the jump was to be made into Lake Erie, he donned a bathing suit, over which the harness was then fitted. As an added precaution for his safety, an inner tube from one of the airplane spare wheels was pressed into service. It was partially inflated, and we tied it around his middle to keep him afloat once he had landed in the lake. Chilson looked at it and then at us, and remarked with a wan smile, "It feels good to have it on, but maybe it will mark the spot where I plunge into the depths." We all laughed at his remark, but it held a vague portent which was not pleasant to think about.

As he climbed into the rear cockpit of the "Jenny" any thoughts he may have harboured of a comfortable trip aloft were at once dispelled. The bulging pack on his back prevented him from sitting down. The only alternative remained for him to turn around, facing towards the tail of the airplane, and then kneel on the seat. In that cramped posture he crouched down as low as possible to avoid the blast of air from the propeller as Russell gave the engine the "gun" and away they went.

Circling as they climbed, they were not long reaching an altitude of 2,000 feet, well out over the lake where the jump had been planned to take place. Fighting the wind as the machine sped through the air, Chilson finally managed to clamber over the side of the cockpit and on to a wing.

As Russell told me later, he too received quite a thrill from the affair when Chilson looked at him with a sort of "good-bye for ever" expression on his face, as he let go his hold on the aircraft, and vanished.

The design of that original back-pack chute did not include a ripcord to manipulate the release of the chute by hand. Instead, there was a fifteen-foot length of quarter-inch-diameter woven rope. One end of it was attached firmly—and I mean firmly—to a strong rigid fitting of the aircraft. The other end of the rope was sewn tightly to a canvas panel on the rear of the parachute pack. The panel kept the parachute snugly in its container until needed. Thread tied tightly through eyelets in the panel and the main container held the two together. It was just as simple as that.

Once a parachutist was ready to launch himself into space, all he had to do was to suppress any qualms in his mind that the chute might not function, and then let go of the airplane, hoping with a prayer on his lips that everything would work as planned. Today this type of jump is used by all airborne paratroopers who jump from an aircraft, and it is known as a static line release.

Chilson's drop was a complete success. As he fell away from the "Jenny," the rope paid out smoothly, ripping the panel clear, and the chute emerged and blossomed without a hitch. We had arranged for a motorboat to be cruising the area where he expected to drop into the lake, and its occupants soon reached him and hauled him aboard.

Crystal Beach was packed solid with American visitors that day It was the Fourth of July, but as the parachute jump had not been publicized or announced in any way it caused no excitement. Thousands on the beaches and in the water never knew it had happened.

A very important development in parachute-making came from Chilson's dip in the lake. The chute he used was fabricated from the best white silk material available, but ordinary cotton thread had been used to sew all the seams. After its immersion in the lake, the chute was a strange thing to behold. The stitching everywhere had slightly shrunk, and some of the seams had taken on the appearance of the puckered lips of a toothless human being. Silk thread went into the making of all later Irvin chutes until the advent of nylon.

Thoroughly water-soaked, the chute and its canvas container were left with us at Crystal Beach to be thoroughly dried out before being returned to Buffalo.

It was then that Russell and I cooked up a little scheme of our own. The weather was very hot at that date, the temperature standing at about ninety during the day, and by mid-morning of July 5th chute and container were thoroughly dry. The puckered effect along the seams was still very much in evidence, but that meant nothing to us.

First we spread out a long wide strip of newspapers on the grass beside our tent. Placing the chute on it, we carefully straightened it out full length, doing the same with the shroud lines, which connect the chute canopy to the harness worn by the jumper.

As we meticulously folded the lines and chute into the container, a separate twenty-foot length of light woven canvas strip went snugly with it. The strip was not attached to the chute in any manner, but its upper end was stoutly sewn to the inside of the panel which in use was pulled away. The design of this ejection method assured instant action when the time came.

By the time we had things figured out how to pack the chute correctly in its container, and had the rip panel in place, the whole thing bulged ominously, but we thought we had done a splendid job and were quite proud of our handiwork.

It was almost mid-afternoon on the 5th when I slipped into my bathing suit and Russell helped me to put on the harness and secure it in place, the welcome addition of the partially blown-up inner tube not being overlooked.   As I climbed laboriously into the rear cockpit I can honestly say I felt more like a deep-sea diver than a prospective parachutist.

As Russell prepared to take off I settled myself on the seat as best I could.   I was also obliged to kneel, facing backward, but as we had removed the seat cushion I was able to crouch much lower than Chilson had done, and the rush of wind did not bother me too much.

We were not long in reaching 1,800 feet in altitude, well out over Lake Erie, but short as the time was my knees hurt like blazes by the time we levelled off.   Although it was a scorching hot day, I was chilled through in my almost naked condition. In my mind, I considered that was the reason for my sudden spells of shivering, but after it was all over, I knew in my heart it was not just the cold wind that had been entirely to blame. The excitement building up had plenty to do with those goose pimples.

When I mentioned that Chilson fought his way out of the cockpit, it was an understatement.   Maybe I did not have the same strong muscles but whatever it was it took all the strength I possessed to hold on, and prevent myself being whipped into space before I was set to go.   The wind from the propeller hit me with terrific force as I emerged into its full blast, the bulky package on my back offering a perfect target for its fury.   Had I lost my grip I would have been swept into the tail section, and what dire results to the plane and occupants might have resulted is anyone's guess.

At last I was clear, standing precariously on the left lower wing but still hanging on like mad, and when I glanced below my stomach muscles cringed as though in the grip of a giant fist. I was then at an age when danger was the least of my thoughts, but if ever a fellow wanted to climb back into the safety of a cockpit, I did at that moment.

We had planned for Don to do a climbing left turn, as I left the machine, to prevent any possibility of myself or the emerging parachute fouling the tail section. Suddenly, I realized Don was doing just that, and I knew the moment had come. Reaching into his cockpit with my left hand for a brief moment we were in touch as our hands met, then I let go.

For a split second I balanced on the wing, and then the rush of wind swept me off, and I plummeted down.

Many times I have been asked how I felt at that moment. I always feel a little sheepish when I have to reply that I don't know, but I don't—things happened just too fast for honest recollections.

What my position was during my brief free fall I cannot say, but the first vivid thing I do remember was the sudden, vicious yank of the harness against my bare shoulders. The red welts I received there reminded me of that moment for days after. I also well remember the ripping sound the chute made when it opened and, for one horrible second after the resounding "froo-o-o-ff" reached my ears, I thought it had burst wide open.

Then there I was, serenely hanging in space, seemingly attached to a giant swing, high above the water. It was a startling experience but one of tremendous exhilaration.

Soon enough I noticed the lake was coming up to meet me in a lazy sort of way, as boats on its surface began to grow larger and larger as I drifted down towards them.

Russell told me afterwards that immediately I left the wing he at once lost sight of me, and as he circled around a terrible thought struck him. He believed I had plunged straight down with an unopened chute. He had planned to take a number of photographs of me as I floated down and had not realized how far I was below him when he started looking for me. Finally he spotted the white chute against the grey background of the lake, and he was hard pressed to catch up with me. With engine power full on, he put the "Jenny" into a steep dive and managed to get close enough to snap one good photo before I reached the surface of the lake.

When I plunged into the lake I went completely under, but the buoyant inner tube yanked me back up, and I shot high out of the water before I again settled back in a normal float. We had not hired a boat for a pick-up but there were several about, and I was soon hauled aboard one by its astonished occupants. I still shivered, but this time for a different reason. Lake Erie is just about the coldest water I have ever experienced. Along the sun-warmed beaches it was wonderful, but well out from shore it seemed like ice-water.

As Don and I sat at supper that night we discussed the entire affair. Quite casually, he said, "You know, Frank, I had some doubts as to whether we had packed the darn thing right." It was then that I confessed that I had thought the selfsame thing.

We looked at each other, and the same thoughts crossed both our minds as the realization struck us of what might have happened if we had "goofed." Then, there would have been no nice drift down to the lake for me. Instead, the malfunctioning chute might easily have trailed behind, droning a death dirge as I hurtled down without a future.

Right then Don and I understood what the risks had been, and without a word we reached out across the table and silently shook hands. There was no need to speak. It was the spontaneous action of two airmen who understood.

In eastern Canada there were several additional outstanding air events with which the redoubtable "Jennies" and their equally worthy pilots should be credited.

One was a flight on July 23, 1919, when pilot Don Russell, of Allied Aeroplanes, Ltd., flew to Buffalo, N.Y., to pick up a passenger in the person of Mr. J. D. Larkin, Jr., and fly him to Crystal Beach, on the Canadian side of Lake Erie. With the accomplishment of the flight Mr. Larkin had become the first paying passenger ever to fly across the International Border.

Another airman, pilot Holmes of Toronto, who had purchased a war-surplus "Jenny," did some risky flying in June, with a photographer installed in the rear cockpit. Together they flew very low over the lip of Niagara Falls, the wheels of the JN4 almost touching the edge of the Horseshoe Falls on the Canadian side as pilot Holmes dived into the gorge beyond.

Then, only a few feet above the water, he proceeded to fly below all of the great bridges linking both sides of the Niagara River. Tremendous air currents aroused by the boiling waters of the gorge so close below pitched the aircraft about in an alarming manner, and they were fortunate to finally fly out over Lake Ontario unscathed, but some magnificent photographs resulted from their daring escapade.

In the Maritimes, pilots Laurie Stevens and L. L. Barnhill established the Devere Aviation Company at Halifax, their entire flying stock in trade being a war-surplus wheel-equipped "Jenny." To draw public attention to their efforts they planned a flight from the Canadian mainland to Prince Edward Island, and on September 24, 1919, they set off from Truro, Nova Scotia, to make the long crossing of Northumberland Strait. Fortune in the guise of a smooth-running engine carried them safely over the wide ocean stretch, and a good landing was made at Charlottetown, P.E.I., where 200 letters they had flown over were at once handed over to the postal authorities for official distribution.

They flew back from Charlottetown to Truro on September 29th, taking along only thirty letters this time, and their return hop was equally successful. Outgoing letters are today valued at $150 each, while the return ones are catalogued at $200 per specimen.

That makes the entire number in a bunch worth the tidy sum of $36,000 if an individual had them all today, but long ago they all vanished into different collections. The irony of it is that neither pilot retained a single envelope to cash in on in the years to come.

Because so many of the JN4 aircraft purchased in Canada directly after World War One were flown in connection with stunting exhibitions or for brief paid-for passenger hops, their use might appear to have been totally confined to that type of flying. It was an era when progress in aviation was not very pronounced, and the few exploits accomplished as true commercial ventures stand out like shining stars.

One of the most pretentious had its beginning in Nova Scotia where the H. V. Green Labrador Expedition of Canada, Ltd. was organized at Annapolis Royal, in 1920.

It was established with the object of going to southern Labrador to undertake a forest survey and to take aerial photographs of a huge tract of virgin timber believed suitable for the manufacture of pulp. The area stretched over some 2,500 square miles back from tide water, beyond Battle Harbour, St. Louis Inlet and Alexis Bay, in southern Labrador. Natural lakes and watercourses, which centred on the area, appeared to make it ideal for getting out the timber once it was cut, and the expedition's purpose was to find out all there was to know on the subject.

The expedition was comprised of thirty personnel, five of whom were pilots, and it was headed by an ex-war pilot, Lieutenant Daniel Owens. The lengthy title of the original company apparently was too much for the newspapers at Annapolis Royal, because the name was soon cut down to the Owen's Survey Expedition, and so it remained until the operations had been completed.

Two Curtiss JN4's were purchased and assigned to the job, one being wheel-equipped while the other was converted for use as a seaplane.

The expedition was well organized, adequately outfitted, and its personnel left Annapolis Royal for Labrador the first week in July, 1920, aboard the S.S. *Granville* and upon reaching Battle Harbour a base was at once established where a suitably-cleared area near the Grenfell Mission buildings presented a good flying field.

The entire project was a costly business, running into a sum close to $200,000 according to reports at the time. Seventy-five thousand dollars is said to have been paid out for aircraft and other equipment. Five thousand gallons of gasoline and 500 gallons of oil for aircraft use were shipped north, together with a mass of necessary supplies and almost enough spare parts to build another complete airplane.

A progressive and pioneer addition towards the safety of flying personnel were three Morse code wireless sets which were used to good effect during the many aerial observations. Their range was somewhat short, being only 125 miles, but it was in keeping with the flying range of the Curtiss "Jennies."

A very happy influence the expedition carried to Labrador was an ice-cream-making machine which was installed aboard the S.S. *Granville*. Aside from its product being enjoyed by all members of the expedition, it brought huge excitement and delight to the Indian children at the Grenfell Mission, none of whom had ever before experienced the joy of eating ice-cream. The Catholic Sisters at the Mission reported that the promise of ice-cream every day had an extraordinary effect on the good behaviour of their young charges, and the Nuns soon dubbed the ice-cream-making equipment "an angelic machine."

Credit is due to all members of the survey crew for a job well done. There were no accidents to the "Jennies," and all work planned proceeded according to schedule.

By the time the survey was brought to a close at the end of August most of the area planned for aerial inspection had been covered and a total of 13,000 photographs had been taken from the air.

The actual finances which sponsored the expedition were from funds of the Southern Labrador Pulp and Lumber Company, Inc., of Boston, Mass., who then owned a ninety-nine-year lease on approximately one and a half million acres of the finest timber land in southern Labrador.

The findings of the Owen's Survey Expedition sparked the beginning of vast pulpwood undertakings in Labrador, repercussions of which have grown to tremendous proportions today, with all due recognition to a couple of sturdy Curtiss "Jennies" and their equally good Canadian pilots, who started the ball rolling so many years ago.

11. The Atlantic Heroes —Alcock and Brown

WHEN MEN FIRST took to the air in balloons, long before the era of power-driven airships and airplanes, the thoughts and hopes of some of the pioneers was to fly across the Atlantic Ocean. A few did try it, using gas-filled balloons and airships, but every one of those attempts ended in failure. Such unwieldy craft were at the mercy of the winds and weather and, coupled with the great distance to be spanned, all such efforts proved fruitless.

Not until 1919 was the North Atlantic Ocean finally vanquished by air. Two British airmen were the heroes of the first nonstop flight across.

With the advent of sturdy-built airplanes, with the ability to fly long distances without stopping to refuel, numerous airmen soon were organizing and planning to try to be the first across just as soon as World War One was over.

The fact that the strong prevailing winds constantly sweep across the Atlantic from west to east influenced the majority of hopeful contestants to start their flight attempts from the North American side. As Newfoundland and Ireland are the two closest land masses directly across the Atlantic, they at once became the focal points for takeoffs and landings.

In the spring of 1919, several airmen shipped their aircraft to Newfoundland to congregate in the vicinity of St. John's where they set up shop, readying their respective machines in preparation for flight attempts across. A coveted prize of ten thousand pounds (approximately $50,000) offered by the English newspaper, *The Daily Mail*, awaited the lucky winner.

On May 18th, the first try from Newfoundland was made by two English airmen, Harry Hawker and K. Mackenzie-Grieve, flying a single-engined Sopwith biplane, aptly named the *Atlantic*. Luck was against them in spite of their sturdy craft. About halfway across their engine began to malfunction and they were obliged to make an emergency landing in the sea. Good fortune did not entirely forsake them because they were able to settle down on the huge seas without going under, and another lucky break was the nearness of the *Mary*, a Dutch ship, the crew of which immediately came to their aid. They were rescued with great difficulty from the storm-tossed waters as their biplane became a battered wreck.

Then in June the electrifying news was flashed around the world that the Atlantic had been flown nonstop.

Two more British ex-war pilots featured in the great event. They were John Alcock and Arthur Whitten Brown, who had commenced their flight from St. John's on June 14, 1919, and in their big twin-engined Vickers Vimy biplane had sped into flying history.

For sixteen hours they battled storms, wind and rain, at times flying for miles on end through vast masses of dense clouds where visibility was nil, and there were no blind-flying instruments on their dashboard. They simply flew by their natural instincts to keep on a level keel, a method of flying which only expert airmen can accomplish. Through the dark hours of that violent storm-tossed night they flew, sitting side by side in an open cockpit where rain and hail battered them time and again.

Once in the blackness they completely lost control of the Vimy when they stalled it unknowingly, and it fell away into a spin. As they spun through space towards the waiting waves both airmen fought the controls to bring the big craft back to level flight. In describing the peril they had been through, Alcock later stated they were almost into the water before they at last gained control. He also mentioned that it was the nearest brush with death he had ever experienced as an airman. Coming from a fighter pilot, not long finished with the risks involved in wartime flying, it proves that the Atlantic incident was a very close call indeed.

Weary but jubilant with success, the airmen finally swept low over the Irish coast, and through the heavy mist which lay over the countryside they began to search for a suitable spot to land. After much circling about they saw what seemed to be a suitable area, near Clifden, so down they went for a landing. The haze had deceived them. No sooner had the wheels of the heavy craft touched down than they sank axle deep, and the Vimy went up on her blunt nose amidst a great crackling of breaking wood and snapping wires. They had landed on a bog, and the staunch nose of the biplane was buried deep in the good Irish muck.

Uninjured, the airmen quickly secured guards to watch their machine, and they at once set off for London. Their arrival at the metropolis touched off a tremendous reception in their honour. Hundreds of thousands of people swarmed through the streets in wild delight, and a dense crowd milled around King's Cross railway station to welcome the airmen on arrival from their great adventure.

As the first airmen ever to span the Atlantic nonstop their achievement was heralded throughout the world, and His Majesty King George V bestowed a knighthood on each of the daring pair in recognition of their splendid accomplishment.

It is a happy thing to be able to record that the Vickers Vimy was not seriously damaged. After being salvaged and put into first class condition it was placed in the South Kensington Museum, at London, where it may still be viewed today. Standing close beside, it is a thrilling experience as you admire its sturdy build and powerful-looking engines, and the realization comes to you that there before you is the first airplane that ever conquered the Atlantic nonstop, and in which two gallant airmen flew to worldwide fame.

For many years after the flight had been accomplished residents of Newfoundland, and particularly of St. John's, discussed ways and means of erecting a suitable memorial to commemorate the exploit, but nothing resulted until 1954. Then a fine stone monument was erected close by the spot from which the Vickers Vimy took off, the unveiling taking place on August 8th with all due ceremony. Built under the joint sponsorship of Newfoundland citizens and the Historic Sites and Monuments Board of Canada, its bronze plaque reveals the reason the monument is there together with brief details telling the story of the great achievement.

12. Wings for Our Forest Patrols

DURING THE CLOSING MONTHS of World War One, a number of large single-engined flying-boats were commissioned for use off Canada's eastern seaboard, their duties consisting of ship convoying and submarine patrols. Designated as HS2L's, their manufacturer's registration lettering, they operated from bases established in Nova Scotia and Newfoundland.

Capable of making wide sweeps out to sea of many hours duration, they each carried a crew of three. They were not fighting aircraft, but a machine gun was mounted on the bow which could be operated by an observer seated in the single front cockpit. The pilot and co-pilot sat side by side in another cockpit farther back between the bow and the biplane wings.

When the war ended, the surplus HS2L flying-boats became available for peacetime flying. Many were pressed into use by the government and others were purchased by civilian flying organizations, to be used with great success on many missions.

The first two HS2L's to become associated with commercial flying in Canada were purchased from the Dominion Government by the St. Maurice Fire Protection Association of Quebec, destined for use in patrolling the forested areas of the St. Maurice Valley. Each aircraft in turn was flown from its wartime base at Dartmouth, Nova Scotia, to Grand Mère on Lac à la Tortue, Quebec, an air distance of 645 miles.

The flights carried the flying-boats over the densely-forested areas of Maine and New Brunswick, and it was the first time in Canada and probably anywhere in the world that such a type of aircraft had made such a lengthy overland flight. The credit for making both trips, a week apart in June, 1919, goes to three people. The pilot was Stuart Graham, the engineer, William Kahre, and the third occupant was Mrs. Graham, who went along for the ride under the title of "official navigator."

The first of those two aircraft to go into patrol service over the wooded forest lands of the St. Maurice Valley received the name of *La Vigilance*, a most appropriate choice. Translated it means watchful or alert. As its crew droned high over the vast timbered areas they were constantly vigilant for a puff of distant smoke rising above the treetops, which meant but one thing—a forest fire.

Radio communication between an airplane and ground stations had not been developed at that date, and immediately a wisp of smoke was spotted the flying-boat was flown back to its base and the fire reported. Men and light fire-fighting equipment always stood by in the dry summer months for instant use, and the aircraft would fly them to the nearest point possible to the fire so that it could be fought at once. Hundreds of fires started by lightning were spotted and brought under control during the first year the HS2L's were used. The immense benefit which airplanes could offer in such work was at once established, and it has grown to tremendous proportions in Canada today.

Following the excellent example set by the St. Maurice company, the Dominion government and several provincial governments soon established their own aerial forest patrols.

The most progressive step in this respect was made by Ontario when the Ontario Provincial Air Service was organized in 1924. They used HS2L's exclusively during their early years of operation, and in that period their pilots covered practically every inch of the thousands of square miles of the Province's vast forest areas.

As forestry flying grew apace many HS2L's were pressed into service for many other types of useful work. Canadian officials bound for remote spots in the wilderness were flown to their destinations or transported out by air, giving up the slow and tiring methods of old which for centuries had consisted in summer of travel either by boat or canoe over tedious routes following inland watercourses. Medical officers were flown to outlying habitations to attend the sick, or members of the Royal Canadian Mounted Police were quickly delivered to isolated settlements when the need arose.

The Indian Affairs Department, realizing the immense time saving which lay in the use of aircraft, soon were requisitioning HS2L flying-boats for the conveyance of their employees to wilderness points. A vast amount of travel time was saved by officials visiting widely-scattered Indian reservations when the annual treaty money payments had to be made, especially in the northern Ontario sections of James Bay and along the southern shore of Hudson Bay. Journeys, which in previous years had required a full summer to complete by water transportation, suddenly became possible in a matter of a few weeks.

Government fishery departments early utilized HS2L's to patrol both eastern and western coastal waters, where fish poaching had become a thriving but illicit business. Boats being used in that unlicensed method of catching fish were extremely difficult to apprehend by the use of surface vessels. Aircraft soon changed all that. On the Pacific coast particularly salmon poaching was rampant, but once a patrol system from the air went into effect the fishermen of that ilk became very rare; the risk of being caught had become too great.

The Canadian Customs Department were also quick to realize the benefit which could be derived by using HS2L's to aid in the prevention of smuggling as applied to passenger ships arriving from the Orient. Narcotics, and particularly opium, were being smuggled into Canada at west coast points in a most ingenious manner, but the use of flying-boats finally put an end to the nefarious business so far as that method was concerned.

Chinese crew members of ocean-going liners were chiefly responsible for the dope smuggling, and the way they worked it was extremely clever. As a ship was nearing Victoria, or Vancouver, buoyant containers of opium would be placed in a sack containing a large amount of salt. After sealing the bag up it would be dropped overside at a designated spot, where a so-called fishing boat would be idling about. Once in the water the weight and density of the salt carried the bag and its contents to the bottom like a stone. Anyone glancing back down the wake of the liner would see nothing suspicious.

Then, as the salt quickly dissolved and washed out through the coarse weave of the bag, the buoyant container would cause the sack to rise to the surface. Watchful eyes aboard the fish boat would spot it and salvage was quickly effected.

Flying-boats would meet the liners when well out at sea and, continually circling back and forth over their course, they were able to spot small vessels which seemed to be hanging around. Then a landing would be made on the water close to them and both boat and occupants would be thoroughly checked. Many arrests resulted and dope-running by that method soon died out.

All through the nineteen-twenties, and well along into the thirties, HS2L flying-boats plied their many missions in Canadian skies. Then, as with all things, they gradually disappeared from use, either from old age or from misadventure, to become just one more airplane of memory. Other and more modern types of course took up where they left off, and the never-ending forest patrols still go on, but the glamour of the early flying years when the HS2L's were the mainstay of such work is now a thing of the past.

13. Perilous Passage

IT WAS QUITE a formidable undertaking. Not only were the airmen instructed to fly from New York to Nome, Alaska, but back again as well. It was a total distance by air of 9,000 miles over some of the wildest mountain areas of the North American continent, and the year was 1920.

When the Alaskan Highway was constructed during World War Two the chain of splendid airfields to Alaska were also established, to be designated by the name of The Northwest Staging Route. The two tremendous undertakings combined cost over fifty-eight million dollars to complete, and they were both built in double-quick time because of the threat of Japanese attack in Alaska.

It seems a long way back to 1920, yet the Alaska air route actually had its beginning that year with the successful completion of a brilliant adventure, known as the First Alaska Air Expedition.

The first knowledge that residents of the Yukon and Alaska received that such a project was under consideration was the arrival at Whitehorse of Captains H. T. Douglas of the U.S. Army Air Service and H. A. Le Royer of the Canadian Air Force. The officers went north by boat in the early summer of 1920, their job being to report on suitable landing-areas in the north. The first spot they selected was at Whitehorse, a 1,650-foot by 375-foot area on the outskirts of the town.

While they were conducting their search, plans for the Expedition were nearing completion at Washington, D.C. The group of airmen selected for the flight (it might better have been called the ordeal) were Captain St. Clair Streett in command, First Lieutenants R. C. Kirkpatrick and C. C. Nutt, Second Lieutenants C. H. Crumrine and E. H. Nelson, Sergeants E. Henriques and J. Long, and Master Electrician J. E. English.

Four two-seated 400 h.p. De Havilland biplanes of British design were selected for the flight, and well they proved their ability to take the tremendously rough usage to which they were subjected.

The Expedition set off from Mitchell Field, Long Island, N.Y., on July 15, 1920, and from that time onward, the men and machines were to wage an almost continuous battle against the elements and rugged terrain until the flight concluded.

Planned stops were at Erie, Pa., Grand Rapids, Mich., Winona, Minn., Fargo and Portal, N.D., Saskatoon, Sask., Edmonton, Alta., Prince George and Hazelton, B.C., Wrangell in Alaska, Whitehorse and Dawson in the Yukon, then Fairbanks and Ruby in Alaska, and finally Nome.

Their return trip to New York was supposed to follow the same route in reverse, but it did not work out that way. Bad weather slowed up their progress time after time, and it was July 25th before they had reached the International Border at Portal and had crossed into Canada. They landed at the McClelland Airfield at Saskatoon on that date and the following day flew on to Edmonton. Knowing the ordeal which lay ahead, with the great barrier of the Rocky Mountains in their path, they took time out to give all four engines a thorough check before leaving on August 1st.

A small makeshift landing-area awaited their coming at Jasper, Alberta, but clever airmen as they were they all managed to get down into it without trouble. The next day the Expedition set off to fly over the high ranges, heading for Prince George in central British Columbia. Three of the airplanes made it flying in formation, although Crumrine's craft blew a tire on landing and then went up on its nose, smashing its propeller.

Captain Streett was hardly out of sight of Jasper, when his engine caught fire, and he lost no time winging back and was able to extinguish it before much damage resulted. Off again an hour later, he reached Prince George as night was closing in, and a deluge of rain which greeted him on arrival did not help matters. When his six colleagues heard the drone of his engine they lighted gasoline flares to guide him in, but he overshot the small runway to end up in the bush with a smashed lower wing.

Strict orders had been issued for all four aircraft to stay together at all times if it was possible to do so, and days went by before the two damaged machines were ready to fly again. To help speed up the work a cabinetmaker from Prince George was hired to help.

While repairs were being made, Streett and Nutt journeyed by train to Hazelton to size up landing prospects there. They found a glum outlook. No suitable spot existed. The only area remotely large enough was on the farm of a Mr. Bierns, and that was a field of oats. They had to make the best of it, so arrangements were made with the owner to have a swathe cut through the oats wide enough and of sufficient length for a plane to land on. The strip was then harrowed and rolled, and was soon as ready as it ever would be for use. A number of Indians from a nearby reserve were hired to help in the undertaking, and one, not liking the job, turned to Captain Streett and said, "You heap smart man, but heap big fool."

At last the repairs to the aircraft at Prince George were completed. On August 13th all four of them took off for Hazelton to make good landings on arrival, after having made British Columbia aviation history by being the first to fly across the Province from east to west. With weather in their favour they refuelled and were off for Wrangell, Alaska, without delay.

The maps they possessed were ordinary topographical ones issued by the government, and they were most unsuited for use from an airman's point of view. Shortly after leaving Hazelton they encountered a dense overcast at five thousand feet. The risk was too great to fly below it or through it, so they went up to a high altitude, beyond where they knew hundreds of hidden mountain peaks lay waiting for any airman foolish enough to fly blind under such conditions. At last, through a rift in the clouds, Streett spotted a river which he was able to identify as the Naas, when he checked with the shape of the Portland Canal which he could see at the same time. Into clearing skies they went on, over the Stewart Arm and the Behm Canal, to finally reach Wrangell.

Good landings were made on the tide flats of Sergieff Island where residents, knowing of their coming, had kept smoke-smudges going to guide them in. The place they landed was a prearranged one, but the airmen had not been informed that the area was available only at low tide. At high tide, it was inundated to a depth of nineteen feet. They were just lucky to arrive when the tide was out.

The 16th saw them set off for Whitehorse, but again Streett was unlucky. All the propellers on the machines were of wood, and a stone nicked one of the blades of the commander's craft, so it had to be smoothed off and balanced, and he did not reach Whitehorse until the following day.

Only twenty-two years before a straining horde of gold-seeking humanity had struggled along the ground, covering the same route which the Expedition followed as they flew over the Chilkoot Pass, better known as the Trail of '98.

As the airman crossed into Yukon Territory from the south, they too made northern history by being the first pilots ever to fly in the Yukon. Throughout the Yukon, August 17th is celebrated as Discovery Day, an annual affair marking the first discovery of gold in the Klondike.

The airmen were anxious to reach Dawson on that date to take part in the celebrations, but only two planes made it right away, one being flown by Kirkpatrick, the other by Nutt.

Crumrine blew a tire on his De Havilland as he was attempting a takeoff from Whitehorse, so Streett stayed behind with him to help make repairs. Late in the afternoon another try was made to get away. Streett took off first without difficulty, but Crumrine's tire again burst. Being in the air, Streett decided not to risk a landing before going on, so he set off for Dawson and there joined his friends to await Crumrine's coming.

With the aid of a local teamster, who supplied reins from a set of harness, the two resourceful airmen left at Whitehorse set about fixing their tire.   First they bound the wheel tightly with a long length of rope, over which they placed the outer tire, lashing it firmly in place with the reins.   It looked all right, and so it proved, for on the 18th they made a getaway and joined the others at Dawson.

The four airmen safely survived the official (and unofficial) "high jinks" at Dawson, and the 19th found them on the wing again, to reach Fairbanks, Alaska, the same day.   The next lap to Ruby was accomplished on the 20th and the final hop to Nome on the 23rd where they rolled to a stop at 5.30 p.m. on the Fort Davis parade ground, almost on the edge of the Bering Sea.

By this time they had logged 55 hours' flying time, had travelled 4,500 air miles and forty days had gone by since they had left New York.   No doubt the Atlantic Ocean seemed a million miles away to them as they stood in the Land of the Midnight Sun.   Perhaps that impression was the reason for their short stay at Nome, because they knew that far away as they were their job was only half done.

On August 26th the few residents of Nome stood by as the four machines rose into the air, vanishing into the distance as the long and arduous trek back began.

By September 3rd they had arrived at Dawson but the season was getting a little late for pioneer flying in that part of the world, with winter storms already brewing.   Flying through bad weather on the 4th, they were fortunate to make White-horse.   By this time each plane held its quota of souvenirs, which included two small husky dog puppies snugly encased in a box in Kirkpatrick's machine.

Bad weather then settled down in earnest and, although they made an attempt to reach Telegraph Creek on the 5th, a dense snowstorm forced them back.   The reason a different route was selected on the return journey was because it followed the north-south telegraph line from Whitehorse to the "outside."   They hoped to be able to make use of it at various points they might stop at on the way to obtain weather reports along the route ahead.

Streett wired Telegraph Creek from Whitehorse, asking them to notify him when weather cleared at their end.   On

September 8th the report came through that things looked good, so the four machines hopped off. It was of no use, dense snow clouds came rolling in over the mountains almost at once and there was nothing for it but to turn back. Kirkpatrick did not show up, but later it was learned he had lost his way and turned up at Wrangell.

Perhaps it was not an accident on his part, but mighty good navigation. *En route* north the handsome young airman had met a young lady at Wrangell and love had blossomed between them, so maybe he took that opportunity of seeing her again before he set off over the mountains for New York.

The three at Whitehorse tried again on the 9th and made it to the Diamond-C Ranch, twelve miles down the Stikine River from Telegraph Creek. Crumrine, still the unlucky one, smashed his craft's undergear when landing in a hayfield, but the group were fortunate in another respect. The only vessel plying the river at the time was a launch, the *Hazel H*, and it so happened it was tied up at the ranch dock when the flyers arrived. When it returned downstream to Wrangell, Streett and Nutt were aboard and were able to pick up spare parts stashed at Wrangell and return with them to the ranch. Crumrine's damaged machine was soon repaired, but numerous attempts to fly south were of no avail against the vast storm clouds and the almost ever-present squalls.

The De Havilland in which Kirkpatrick and English were flying kept going and reached Edmonton on September 16th. He was ordered to go on in not too much of a hurry as the weather was worsening and no one knew when the other three aircraft would make Edmonton.

In the meantime the grounded airmen at Telegraph Creek invented an ingenious method for receiving a good weather report from the telegraph station should one come. The village where the operator was, stood some twelve miles from the ranch, so two men were stationed at set times daily on heights of land, one some distance from the ranch and the other near the telegraph station. If a good weather report came in from the south the man at the village was to set off a charge of dynamite. When the second man near the ranch heard the blast he in turn was to set off another which would be heard by the airmen.　It was a tedious wait before at last the welcome explosion was heard. The noise had scarcely stopped echoing back and forth from the surrounding hills before all three aircraft were in the air high-tailing it for Hazelton.　It was a rough flight but they made it and, taking advantage of better weather prevailing in the more southerly latitude, they were able to push on, first to Prince George and then to Edmonton, but it was October 8th when they arrived at the Alberta city.

From then onward it was fairly plain sailing, and they caught up with Kirkpatrick along the way where he had awaited their coming.

The big day came on October 20th, when all four machines flew out of the western sky to a landing on Mitchell Field, N.Y., ninety-seven days after their departure the previous July, and the long grind was over.　The average logged flying time for each De Havilland was 112 hours.

In his lengthy report of the flight to U.S. Army Headquarters Captain Streett stated, "The route to Alaska is not feasible until bases are established along the way."

It took many years and the outbreak of World War Two before his words became an established fact.　Although in 1934 the Canadian firm of United Air Transport Ltd. had begun charter flying from Edmonton to the Yukon, their landing-fields along the way left much to be desired.

In 1939 the Canadian government set aside funds for a survey of the route, with the object of building better facilities, but little progress had been made when war broke out.

Then the Canadian-United States Permanent Joint Board of Defence was appointed in 1940 and actual construction began, resulting in the Alaskan Highway and the fine chain of airfields which now serve the route between Edmonton and Alaska.

14. The First Trans-
Canada Air Mail

DURING THE TIME the First Alaska Air Expedition was being planned in the United States Canada's own Air Board was not just sitting back twiddling its thumbs.

They, too, were working on a pretentious undertaking, drawing up all the details connected with a flight from Halifax to Vancouver. In sponsoring the project it was their desire to learn what the possibilities were for the carriage of mail across Canada from coast to coast.

All of the pilots and the ground personnel connected with the flight were drawn from the newly-formed Canadian Air Force. The Royal prefix by which we know the Force today was not then in use, and was not added until April 1, 1924, when Royal Canadian Air Force became the official title.

The aircraft allocated for use with the undertaking from Winnipeg westward were two-seated wheel-equipped De Havilland biplanes, each fitted with a 400 h.p. engine. They were shipped by rail to the prairie destinations from which they were to go into action when their turn came.

All of Canada's military airplanes carried registration lettering at that time, exactly as did civilian craft, and perhaps to give the project a more commercial touch all of the pilots wore civilian clothes instead of their regulation uniforms.

The original plan was for a two-seater Fairey seaplane to make a nonstop flight from Halifax to Winnipeg. The machine was one which had been financed and specially built in England by private enterprise, and had then been shipped to Newfoundland with the intention of using it on a trans-Atlantic flight. That project had been cancelled after the successful Atlantic crossing by Alcock and Brown, the Fairey being placed in storage until acquired by the Canadian government.

For the Canadian flight attempt the Fairey was shipped from Newfoundland to Vickers Limited at Montreal, and Major Basil D. Hobbs, who had been detailed to fly it, supervised its preparation. Tests after the seaplane had been rigged were not too satisfactory, as it would not lift from the St. Lawrence River with the extremely heavy load of fuel it contained. After much delay, Hobbs and his passenger, Lieutenant-Colonel Robert Leckie, set off from Montreal on October 4th, heading for Halifax.

Fifteen miles short of Fredericton, New Brunswick, engine trouble obliged them to make a landing on the St. John River, near the city. The river was in flood at the time and they were swept downstream at a fast clip without steerage of any kind. Fortunately they drifted under a high bridge and the airmen were able to make their craft fast to it until they could effect adjustments to the engine and get it going again. They reached Halifax on the 5th, and preparations at once got under way to take off for Winnipeg.

Both were airmen of long experience, but their combined efforts and knowledge could not induce the machine to lift from the sea with a full load of fuel. Flight plans then were modified, and with a lighter load of gasoline they planned to fly to Ottawa nonstop.

The ambitious trans-Canada flight started on October 7, 1920, and with the airmen went a small pouch containing a number of letters from Mayor J. S. Parker of Halifax, addressed to government, provincial and civic officials along the route. As the seaplane skimmed low over Saint John mail was dropped, addressed to His Worship the Mayor. They might just as well have delivered it in person because they were scarcely away from the place when trouble plagued them again. The cowling broke loose, carrying with it some engine oil pipes, so down they went to another landing on the St. John River. They were not so lucky this time. The heavily-laden craft proved too much of a burden on the pontoon struts as it settled none too lightly on the water. The whole thing buckled and in the resultant crack-up the unfortunate Fairey became a total loss.

Uninjured, both pilots were quickly rescued by people who put out from shore in small boats. Quite undaunted, the airmen requisitioned another aircraft, doing so by phone to Halifax, and a regular HS21 service flying-boat was rushed to their aid.

Hobbs and Leckie immediately took over when it arrived, and late in the afternoon of the 7th they carried on, to reach Rivière du Loup on the St. Lawrence River, doing so in the pitch dark and in a driving rain.

A big F3 twin-engined flying-boat, originally built for war-time Atlantic patrol duty, had been flown downriver from Montreal to await their coming. Its pilot, Captain H. A. Wilson, took over the HS2L and flew it back to Halifax, while Hobbs and Leckie set off in the F3 on October 8th, heading for Ottawa. An additional crew member joined them at this time, Air Foreman Mechanic Charles Heath, who was to act as engineer.

On arrival at the nation's capital, the airmen had 820 miles behind them, and when they took off for Winnipeg on the 9th Captain G. O. Johnson became the fourth crew member, to act in the capacity of navigator.

Much of the long route to Winnipeg had never heard the drone of an airplane in the sky up to that date. North Bay, on Lake Nipissing, was their first objective, and after a refuelling stop there they carried on over the densely-wooded country to Sault Ste. Marie, landing on the St. Mary's River at 5.00 p.m.

Plans were to fly the mail across Canada as quickly as possible, so without delay they fuelled up and were on their way, with the intention of flying the long trip over Lake Superior during the moonlight hours. They had not been long in the air when a pall of fog began to hide the landscape below. So in the

interest of safety a landing was made at the mouth of the St.
Mary's River, where they anchored the flying-boat close to shore
and spent the night.

The 10th was a Sunday, and at sunrise they were off again
and made the first crossing of Lake Superior by air.

By the time they had stopped at Kenora, Ontario, for another
refuelling and had flown on to Winnipeg night had fallen.
They reached the Red River, north of the city, and a landing was
made at Selkirk, some miles short of their destination. They
almost met with disaster when an anchored dredge suddenly
loomed up out of the gloom and the rising mists. As they
touched down on the water the wing tip of their machine missed
it with only inches to spare.

Leckie and Hobbs then travelled by a convenient electric
railway from Selkirk and turned the precious mail bag over to
Captain Home-Hay at St. Charles Aerodrome, west of Winnipeg.
Home-Hay was all set to go with his De Havilland and his
passenger, Lieutenant-Colonel A. Tylee, commanding officer
of the C.A.F., who took charge of the bag of mail.

Daylight was still hours away on October 11th when the
plane set off from Winnipeg, the thunder of its powerful engine
reverberating deeply as it climbed steadily westward over the
sleeping countryside.

It was the only incident I was privileged to witness in connection with the 1920 trans-Canada flight, as I was on the staff of
the Canadian Aircraft Company at the time, and it was their
airfield the airmen used while at Winnipeg. I was one of the
few shivering spectators who stood by to watch their pre-dawn
takeoff and one thing impressed me greatly—the determination
shown by all personnel who took part to keep on the move westward without delay. Storm or shine, day or night, meant little
to them providing the weather allowed them to fly at all.

All went well with Home-Hay and Tylee until they were over
Regina at 8.30 a.m., when without warning their engine began
to act up, so down they went to a landing on the outskirts of
the city. Unable to make quick repairs, a rush S.O.S. telegram
was sent to Moose Jaw where a relay plane was standing by.

John A. D. McCurdy, the
first pilot to fly an
airplane in Canada.

Courtesy Gross, Chicago

The *Silver Dart*, with pilot John McCurdy at the controls,
being wheeled into position on the frozen surface of
Bras d'Or Lake, Nova Scotia, just before the historical first
flight of an airplane in Canada, February 23, 1909.

Courtesy Lieutenant H. Benner

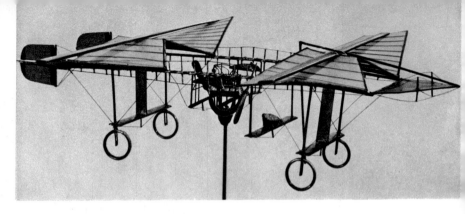

Model of William Gibson's *Twin-plane* made by the author, which is now on permanent display in the National Air Museum, Smithsonian Institution, Washington, D.C.

Courtesy Smithsonian Institution

William Gibson's famous airplane engine on display in the Aeronautical Museum of the National Research Council at Ottawa.

Courtesy National Research Council, Ottawa

William Gibson's Multi-plane on exhibit at the "Made in Canada" fair, held in Vancouver, B.C., June, 1911. Twelve men standing on its framework convincingly demonstrate the craft's structural strength.

Courtesy William W. Gibson

William Wa
Gibson, outstar
pioneer in the fie
Canadian avi

Charles Hamilton's "Aerial Clipper,"
the first airplane to fly
at any point in western Canada.

Courtesy W. Templeton

Sixteen-year-old Larry Lesh of
Montreal in full flight in his own-
made glider.

Charles Willard's *Golden Flyer* at the
Scarboro Beach Fair Grounds,
Toronto, in September, 1909.   Note
the wooden track in which the front
wheel fitted to guide the craft
along the confined take-off area.

Courtesy Al. Martin

Cecil Peoli delights the people of Saint John, New Brunswick, with his flights in the *Red Devil*.   Here, on the left, the first flight gets under way on August 31, 1912.

Courtesy Horace Porter

Eugene Ely beside his fragile machine, shortly before he battled against the strong prairie winds at Winnipeg, in 1910.

Canada's first woman air passenger, Mrs. Olive Stark, with her
pilot husband, all set for the ride which carried her to fame.

The start of Miss Labatt's flight with pilot Walter Brookins, at Port
Stanley, Ontario, when she became the first woman air passenger
in eastern Canada.

Mrs. Alys McKey Bryant,
with the airplane she used
to become the first woman pilot
to fly in Canada, July 31, 1913.

Courtesy Alys McKey Bryant

The "Jenny," Curtiss JN4 two-seater biplane. This is the type of aircraft used exclusively by the R.F.C., and the R.A.F., in Canada, for training purposes during World War One, and widely used by civilian pilots in Canada after the war.

John Alcock and Arthur Brown piloted this twin-engined Vickers Vimy biplane on the first nonstop flight across the Atlantic Ocean, June, 1919.

Courtesy Sir Arthur Whitten Brown

John Alcock (*left*) and Arthur Brown (*right*), the first men to conquer the Atlantic Ocean by air.

Courtesy Sir Arthur Whitten Brown

The single-engined HS2L flying-boat, a type which was used for pioneering forest fire patrol and other useful purposes in Canada after World War One.

Courtesy Mrs. Dora Scott

Captain Streett, leader of the 1920 "New York to Nome and back again" flight, is congratulated by General Pershing on the successful completion of the 9,000-mile air journey.

Courtesy Brigadier General St. Clair Streett

The four De Havilland biplanes of the First Alaska Air Expedition during their brief stop-over at Dawson, Yukon Territory, on their way to Nome, Alaska, from New York in 1920.

Courtesy H. W. Firth

The *Thunder Bird* takes off from Winnipeg, bound for The Pas, October 15, 1920, on the first commercial passenger flight into the Canadian hinterland.

The De Havilland biplane at Revelstoke, during its flight from Calgary to Vancouver, in connection with the trans-Canada air-mail flight made by personnel and machines of the Canadian Air Force in October, 1920.

Courtesy E. Dickey

The first two airplanes ever to penetrate into the Northwest
Territories—the *Vic* (above) and the *Rene* (below).   Both machines
were single-engined all-metal Junkers monoplanes, owned by
Imperial Oil Limited.

Courtesy Dr. Theo Link

During many flying missions in Canada the hull of this Vickers
Viking flying-boat dipped into both the Atlantic and Pacific Oceans,
as well as a great many lakes and watercourses throughout the
country.

Courtesy J. Scott Williams

Pushing through heavy floe ice, ships of the sealing fleet set off
from St. John's, Newfoundland, in March, 1924. The fully-rigged
Baby Avro can be seen perched astern of the S.S. *Eagle* in the
foreground.

Courtesy Ernest Maunder

"Wop" May gets set in the front cockpit of the Avro Avian as the engine warms up in zero weather before the historical mercy flight which he and Vic Horner made from Edmonton to Fort Vermilion in January, 1929.

Mrs. Esmée Cruickshank and her
pilot husband, Andy, with the
Queen of the Yukon in its
midwinter makeshift tent "hangar"
at Mayo, Yukon Territory.

Courtesy Esmée Cruickshank

The famous Gipsy Moth, CF-AAA,
which was flown across Canada
and back on two occasions by its
owner, General Sir James
MacBrien.

The Tiger Moth, a type of
machine in which R.C.A.F. trainees
received elementary flying
instruction during World War Two.
Many civilian pilots also learned
to fly in Moths.

Courtesy H. Parker

Paratroopers disgorging from an R.C.A.F. Fairchild "Packet" of the Transport Command during routine training in Canada. The "Packet" is a modern version of the "flying boxcar."

Courtesy Department of National Defence

left top   Squadron Leader A. E. Godfrey (*left*) and Sergeant Major M. Graham of the R.C.A.F. with the Fairchild seaplane which they flew from Ottawa to Vancouver, September, 1928.

Courtesy Canadian Government Motion Picture Bureau

left middle   One of the two Fokker Universals purchased by Western Canada Airways at the start of their illustrious flying career in Canada. It is seen at the makeshift company office at Pine Ridge, Ontario, during the Red Lake gold rush in 1927.

Courtesy H. A. "Doc" Oaks

left bottom   The Canadian-operated Junkers monoplane, CF-ARM, the original craft to be named a "flying boxcar," a nickname applied to all large air freighters today.

Courtesy W. B. Burchall

The German Junkers monoplane, *Bremen*, being dismantled on Greenly Island after its three-man crew had made flying history by being the first to fly the North Atlantic nonstop in a westerly direction.

Courtesy Romeo Vachon

Bert Hinkler with his De Havilland Puss Moth at Toronto, 1931.

Courtesy De Havilland Aircraft of Canada Ltd.

The sky giant from England, the R-100, casts its vast shadow on Montreal's St. Hubert Airport during its brief visit to Canada in 1930.

Courtesy Department of National Defence

The *Robert Bruce* receives last-minute adjustments in the Short Brothers' Rochester plant, near London, England, before the start of John Grierson's 4,570-mile air journey, via Greenland and Canada, to New York.

Courtesy John Grierson

The De Havilland Dragon Rapide airplane, *Trail of the Caribou*, which Leonard Reid and James Ayling flew nonstop from Wasaga Beach, Ontario, to Heston Airport, England, in August, 1934.   *Courtesy James Ayling*

The undignified ending in a Nova Scotian bog after Beryl Markham's splendid flight from Oxford, England, in her Percival Gull monoplane, Messenger.

Courtesy C. G. Rogers

Beryl Markham, the only woman ever to fly solo across the North Atlantic Ocean from east to west.

One of the PBY Cansos owned by the Canadian company, Aeromagnetic Surveys Limited.   A crew of seven highly skilled men operate the craft and keep check on its numerous instruments as it prospects for minerals, trailing its bomblike electromagnetometer behind.

Courtesy Hunting Associates Limited

Winter touches the Canadian landscape below as this Harvard
two-seater training plane of the R.C.A.F. carries out its mission with
a solo trainee at the controls.

Courtesy Department of National Defence

Caught by winter conditions in the high north, this DC-3 has its wheel
undergear changed to skis right out in the open with zero temperatures
prevailing. A gasoline-operated heater is connected to both engines
to keep them warm and prevent freezing.

A four-engined Lancaster of the
R.C.A.F. seen in full flight.

Courtesy Department of National Defence

One of the Canadian-built four-
engined North Star passenger
aircraft used so extensively by
Canada's larger airlines and by
the R.C.A.F.

Courtesy Department of National Defence

A float-equipped
Norseman aircraft
owned by Pacific
Western Airlines,
Limited, and used
trucking over
Canada's aerial
highways.

*Courtesy Pacific Western
Airlines Ltd.*

The De Havilland Otter, float-equipped and in full flight.
Courtesy De Havilland Aircraft of Canada Ltd.

The versatile De Havilland-built Beaver, equipped
with a combination wheel-ski landing-gear, so well
adapted to winter flying in Canada.
Courtesy De Havilland Aircraft of Canada Ltd.

Owned by the Canadian firm of Okanagan
Helicopters Limited, the world's largest civilian
operators of rotary wing aircraft, this big Sikorsky S55
is seen delivering a one-thousand-pound load
of metal pipe to a location high in the mountains of
British Columbia.　　*Courtesy Okanagan Helicopters Limited*

Just like huge vampire bats, from which their name
stems, these three single-seater Vampire jets
of the R.C.A.F. are in a formation flight position
termed "In line astern."

Courtesy Department of National Defence

The Fairey Rotodyne, a
true aerial passenger
bus, which Okanagan
Helicopters Limited plan
to put into service in 1960
in British Columbia, on a
run between the cities
of Vancouver and Victoria.

Courtesy the Fairey Aviation Co. Ltd·

A Silver Star in the sky. The popular two-seater T-33 jet trainer aircraft used by the R.C.A.F. The large torpedo-shaped pods at either wing tip are auxiliary fuel tanks.

Courtesy Department of National Defence

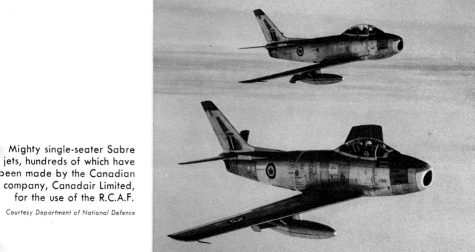

Mighty single-seater Sabre jets, hundreds of which have been made by the Canadian company, Canadair Limited, for the use of the R.C.A.F.

Courtesy Department of National Defence

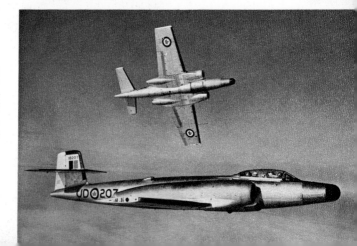

The fast twin-jet Avro CF-100 Canuck, used in numbers by the R.C.A.F. as an intercepter aircraft for the protection of Canada's frontiers.

Courtesy Department of National Defence

The English-built Viscount, first turboprop-engined airliner to be placed in operation on regular passenger-carrying service anywhere in the world. Many of these 300-mile-an-hour aircraft are now in use.

Courtesy Trans-Canada Airlines

"The Whispering Giant," Bristol Britannia airliner, capable of flying 6,000 miles nonstop at 400 miles an hour with 133 persons aboard in its spacious pressurized interior.

Courtesy Canadian Pacific Railway

The De Havilland Comet III in full flight. Numerous records were made by this four-engined jet airliner as it was flown around the world in 1955 by Captain John Cunningham on a combined test and demonstration mission.

Courtesy De Havilland Aircraft of Canada Ltd.

Manned by Captain Cudamore and Sergeant Young, it was soon on the wing and, upon reaching Regina, Home-Hay and Tylee took the seats vacated by them, gave the engine the "gun" and went booming away for Calgary. To greet them at Bowness Park, where they landed, west of the city, was Captain G. A. Thompson with another De Havilland in readiness for the vital flight over the Rocky Mountains.

Weather had become increasingly hostile and winter's edge had already reached the mountaintops, where snowstorms were a daily menace to any airman or aircraft possessed with the audacity of pitting their skill against them. Not until the 13th did the weather appear to clear sufficiently to give the airmen a reasonable excuse for proceeding westward, although reports from along the route they were to follow stated "Dense clouds, with snow."

They flew up the great mountain-girt valley of the Bow River, passing high over Banff, on to Glacier and the Kicking Horse Pass, *en route* to Revelstoke, where they were spotted going over an hour and a half out of Calgary. By this time they had already entered the book of fame by being the first airmen to master the mighty range of the Selkirks by air, but more was to come. After they lost sight of Revelstoke the weather decided to take a hand and closed down all around them.

People on the ground at Vernon, B.C., heard the sound of their engine high up in the overcast but the airmen by that time were flying blind. It is an area of massive peaks in all directions, and no place for a wandering airplane without eyes to see with. It must have seemed an eternity after they had turned back before they were lucky enough to spot Revelstoke below through a break in the storm. Losing no time, they stuck the nose of the De Havilland into the gap and went down to a landing on the Sam Crowe Ranch, three miles south of the town.

The 14th brought a dismal outlook, with vast masses of storm clouds completely encircling the valley in which Revelstoke lies. The ceiling reached down the slopes of the mountains almost to the valley floor and there was no getting away that day. On the

15th a patch of blue sky showed through a break in the overcast, high over Eagle Pass to westward in the direction the airmen wished to go.   Good-byes to freshly made friends at Revelstoke were brief, and just before noon the De Havilland lifted out of the valley and vanished over the heights.   Minutes later the clouds settled down again in gloomy masses, staying that way for over a week, so how lucky the airmen were to get away when they did can easily be understood.

High overhead but unseen to the people of Salmon Arm, B.C., the throb of the engine was heard as the airmen flew through the storm which had brewed.   They kept to an accurate course—proof enough of their navigational abilities—and an hour and a quarter out of Revelstoke they had landed at Merritt, B.C., having had enough buffeting and danger for one day. Storm clouds were everywhere with snow falling almost hourly, and their route over the coast range of mountains by way of the Coquihalla Pass was completely obscured.

Not until the 17th did the semblance of a break come, although conditions were still extremely bad.   The airmen decided to take a chance and made it over the pass to finally spot the Fraser River below.   On this lap of their flight an experience occurred which held the risk of death every moment.   As they flew towards the Pacific coast the overcast grew lower and lower until they were obliged to go down into the winding course of the river itself, flying only a few feet above the surface.   They sped along the valleys and through the high canyons in this hectic manner, mile after mile, turning and twisting with every bend as the cloud cover above pinned them down.   Engine failure, with a consequent forced landing, would have spelled sudden and complete disaster.   At last, through the driving rain, the small village of Agassiz was seen to starboard, and they went down to a landing in a sodden field to learn just where they were and to obtain additional fuel.   They had left Merritt at 9.50 a.m. and by 11.00 a.m. Thompson had put the craft down to a landing on the rain-soaked infield of the Brighouse Park racetrack on Lulu Island, on the outskirts of Vancouver.

The rain still fell in torrents, beating a heavy tattoo on the taut surfaces of the wings, sounding for all the world like the roll of drums—nature's way perhaps of offering homage to two weary airmen at the conclusion of Canada's first trans-continental flight. The total distance covered by all aircraft used was computed by the Air Board at 3,265 air miles, made in a flying time of 45 hours, over an elapsed time of ten days. Considering the time of year, the weather involved and the fact that it was a pioneer effort, it was good going.

The air-mail increased somewhat from the original letters which started from Halifax as numerous others were added to the mail bag at various stops for delivery at Vancouver.

Very few of those "first flight" envelopes have survived, but the archives of the city of Vancouver possesses one complete set, and a few others are scattered about the world in the hands of collectors.

During a luncheon at Winnipeg held shortly after the entire flight had been completed, one brief remark made by Lieutenant-Colonel Leckie is certainly worthy of print: "The trans-Canada flight is not an attempt to go after a record, or do 'stunts.' It is merely a demonstration of the feasibility of using the air route for the carriage of mails across Canada. The flying time will show that the trip can be made much more rapidly by air than by any other means, and succeeding trials will be even more successful."

They were prophetic words, but it required almost two decades for them to become an established fact. It was not until March 1, 1939, that the carriage of mail by air, east and west, became a daily affair in Canada. With its inauguration by Trans-Canada Air Lines on that date it has now grown to immense proportions, proving beyond all doubt that Leckie's utterance, and the faith the Canadian Air Board held in the development of air-mail, was the result of a sound, farsighted, glimpse into the future.

15. The "Thunder Bird"

ON OCTOBER 15, 1920, an airplane set off from Winnipeg, Manitoba, the destination of its three occupants being The Pas, a small village in the northern hinterland, 500 miles north of Winnipeg. Chartered and accomplished without pre-flight arrangements, it became the first "bush" flight into the northland, triggering the true start of modern air transport throughout that whole vast area.

I am going to recount this story in the first person, for at the time I was on the staff of Canadian Aircraft Company of Winnipeg and it fell to my lot, together with another pilot, to make the flight.

When the call came through from our downtown office for pilot Hector Dougall and me to ready our Avro biplane for a passenger flight, we figured it was just another routine hop to a nearby town. When we learned that our destination was The Pas, we looked at each other in surprise and changed our minds in a hurry. No airplane had ever flown up into that wilderness before.

Consulting the inadequate maps we had, we realized the journey would present quite a challenge. We learned that our passenger was a Mr. Frank Stanley, a fur buyer, and that he had paid $475 to be landed safely at The Pas.

That was big revenue for those days. As flying was our business, if he had said "Vladivostok" or "Valparaiso" our reaction would have been much the same. I guess Dougall and I would both have said in close harmony, "Okay, let's go!"

Shortly after Mr. Stanley reached our St. Charles Aerodrome on the morning of the 15th we had him comfortably installed in the plane. On the dot of 11.00 a.m. we sped down the field and were airborne. Possibility of forced landings along the first part of our journey didn't bother us. It was over the Manitoba farmlands, which were ideal for such emergencies. It was the second half which held the unknown quantity. What we would encounter was anyone's guess. It was rough country for a wheel-equipped airplane to penetrate.

Perfect weather prevailed as we headed northwest. The sun and ourselves were alone in the great blue sky. The fields and bushlands below dressed in their autumn hues looked like a huge varicoloured Persian carpet.

Our first planned stop was the town of Dauphin, 296 miles from Winnipeg. At that period of doubtful engine reliability, things didn't always work out just right. We were flying high over the farming community of Gladstone when our first spot of trouble developed.

The Avro, Dougall and I had been a close team for many weeks before The Pas junket began. We had roamed the prairies far and wide, putting on aerobatic exhibitions and carrying passengers. All too well did we know our engine with its unpredictable tantrums. As rotary motors were so prone to do, it suddenly began to act up. The familiar bloop, bloop-bloop coming from the exhaust ports indicated only one thing—ignition trouble. With engine revs dropping at an alarming rate, it meant back to earth for us. In a long lazy glide we settled down to a field quite close to the town. An hour slipped by before we had spare spark plugs installed and were once again airborne.

From 6,000 feet we had an impressive view of the distant stretch of Lake Manitoba, spreading far to the rim of the northern horizon. To the west, dwarfed by the distance and our height, the Riding Mountains with their forest-clad sides looked like huge mounds of moss.

The strong headwind we had encountered, coupled with our enforced stop, put us two hours behind schedule by the time we made Dauphin where a surprise was in store. All of the land surrounding the place had recently been under the influence of the plow.   Not a single grassy pasture showed for miles around. It was all part of our business, so down we went to a bumpy stop among the furrows close to town.

From much experience we knew that only a brief wait beside our aircraft would draw crowds of people, and soon they were tearing along the road towards us, one car after another.   Airplanes were still a rarity in most outlying communities in 1920. In a short time the three of us were being driven into Dauphin by a generous citizen.

With refuelling arrangements made, we decided to refuel ourselves.   Our sojourn in a local cafe took much longer than intended, playing heck with our time plans.   We still had 107 miles to go to reach Swan River.   It was there we had planned to stay the night, and we realized we would be lucky to make it before dark.

The landscape below was becoming more densely sprinkled with bush with every mile, impressing on us the fact that the open farmlands were being left behind.   Along this stretch the forested mass of the Duck Mountains obliged us to follow a course due north before finally turning west for Swan River.   The wind had fallen and we made good flying time.

Night comes early in that latitude at that time of the year. As we approached Swan River and the twinkling lights from the town were all we could see through the gloom, we decided to land a mile from our destination.   It was far too risky to go on.   We landed in a stubble field as darkness closed in all around us. Securing the aircraft with equipment we always carried, we set off to walk the final stage of the journey.   As we trudged and stumbled along that rutted country road in the blackness, it seemed a strange climax to a busy day.   We registered at the hotel, and the next morning awoke to find the weather completely changed.

Under a leaden overcast great masses of filthy-looking clouds scudded fast before a stiff north wind.   The ceiling was low and visibility bad.   The chill breath of winter was suddenly in the air, and the rain came down in torrents.   We obtained gasoline and refuelled the airplane between squalls, but the prospect for getting away looked poor. By 1.30 p.m., however, it seemed to be letting up, so we decided to make a getaway.

Few people in Swan River ever knew they had had three aerial visitors. When we set off with Hudson Bay Junction as our next destination there was not a single soul on hand to see us off. Our route now lay along the eastern fringe of the unseen Porcupine Mountains before we could with safety turn west to the Junction. What a vicious ride we had. No sooner had we lost sight of Swan River than the storm broke all around us. Time and again we were obliged to change our compass course in order to dodge wild flurries of snow. It was an anxious time then for the country had become wild in the extreme, covered with stands of tamarack trees, lakes and muskegs.

During one lull in the storm we were treated to a wonderful experience. A huge flight of Canada geese winged past heading south. It was a magnificent sight, but it boded no good for us. It meant but one thing, winter in the high north was fast sealing the land and water in its icy grip.

Every moment of that hop to the Junction we were tossed and buffeted about, and we were mighty lucky to hit the place right on the nose. Our joy was short-lived. As we flew around in ever-widening circles looking for somewhere to land, we received a mild shock. No cultivated area was to be found in any direction. Our astonishment imparted also a feeling of despair. We had been in the air over two hours and our fuel supply had diminished to the point where we could not continue to The Pas, still 89 miles to the north. Only virgin bush, lakes and muskeg met our eyes as we searched in vain. Swinging back to the village we took our chance on a reed-covered area, a most uninviting landing spot if ever there was one.

As the wheels took the weight they sank axle deep. There was a tremendous jolt and we were yanked to a sudden stop. It was touch and go, and I for one thought we were going to flip over onto our back. The tail shot up behind at a high angle and then fell back. The tough ash skid of the landing-gear had saved the day.

Almost every man, woman, child and dog from the village came on the run. It was a great day for them.

When we climbed out of the bogged-down craft it was almost four in the afternoon. With a couple of hours' daylight left we set to in the pouring rain to get our plane from the muskeg. There was bush-covered higher ground close by, and many willing hands. Axes appeared like magic, and soon a wide swathe was slashed through the undergrowth and small trees. Dougall sat in the machine with his hand on the throttle and, with the prop going like mad and men hauling on the wings, we finally extricated the Avro from its quagmire.

We were dog tired and repaired to the local "hotel" for food and rest. The latter was late in coming that night, the good people of the village entertained us and it was long after midnight before we slept.

Happily the 17th, a Sunday, found the sun shining again and—better for us—a south wind was blowing. After breakfast we sized things up to plan how we hoped to become airborne. Finally we decided to choose the village's only street and to use it as a runway. We moved the plane to the north end, giving us a takeoff strip of about 75 yards. It was desperately short but there was nowhere else.

The answer to our request for gasoline really laid us low. "Gas," the people echoed, "we don't have any, there are no cars in this neck of the woods!" We found out then that the Junction had no road connection with the rest of the world. There was just the railway, over which a train ran once a week— maybe!

While we were discussing what a jam we were in, the news of our plight reached the ears of an elderly Chinaman who was the owner of the village cafe and laundry. He offered us two four-gallon cans of good high-test stuff. It was gasoline he had shipped in strictly for use in gasoline lamps. It was such a windfall we almost hugged him.

By 3.30 in the afternoon we were all set to go. With maybe a fifty-fifty chance we would make it out of there. The takeoff was not a pleasant prospect, so we fastened our safety belts with more than ordinary precaution. A dozen husky men hung onto the wing struts until the engine revved up full blast. They let go at our signal and we shot away at a fast clip. The runway went by with a rush, the wheels slashing through undergrowth as we lifted clear at the street's end just in time.

A smash-up still seemed imminent. Tall pines beyond the slashed area swept our lower wing with their top branches before we were in the clear. Then we reached for altitude until we levelled off at 3,000 feet.

The tension gripping Dougall and myself fell away once the crisis was over. With Mr. Stanley it was different. Nothing seemed to bother him at all, he took everything for granted. I guess he was a true man of the north.

For man's first glimpse of the vast hinterland from the air visibility was perfect. To far horizons the jumbled maze of land and water spread out in all directions. One of nature's intricate jigsaw puzzles lay below—the browns, greens and greys blending together in perfect harmony. Low in the western sky the sinking sun cast its shimmering reflection on a myriad of lakes and watercourses. It was an inspiring and never-to-be-forgotten sight. Once, far below, we spotted the tiny V ripples cut by the bow of a speck-like canoe as its owner paddled across an unnamed lake.

With the strong tailwind pushing us along, we made the 89 miles to The Pas in the quick time of forty-two minutes. News of our coming had been relayed by telegraph to the town, and a large crowd of whites and Indians were on hand to welcome us in.

Mayor Stitt and his aldermen were there to extend official greetings, and on the Monday a banquet was tendered us to mark the arrival of the first plane north. It was a wonderful time for Mr. Stanley. He was the hero of the hour. As the first passenger ever to fly into the north country, he had suddenly become focused in the spotlight of fame.

Indians came from their reservations for miles around to view the modern wonder in which men could fly. Few approached the machine very close but one elderly Cree, braver than most, lay on his back under a wing and just looked and looked. Curious, I asked him what interested him so much. His reply was an eye-opener. "Me just trying to find out how Thunder Bird stay up in sky."

His choice of name for our Avro struck us as most appropriate. So on the 19th a little ceremony was held and the Mayor officially christened our craft *The Thunder Bird*. None of us then realized that the puny echoes from our plane's engine would rise and swell into the immense proportions now developed by northern flying.

One thing I do know, however. Although staunch G-CABV has long ago passed into the strange oblivion which engulfs aged aircraft, its memory should not be forgotten. A sturdy ship, it made air history, bestowing a lasting blessing on an isolated and lonely country by bringing wings to the northland.

16. *"Rene" and "Vic" Were Illustrious Twins*

THIS STORY STARTS OUT with an international aspect, because two single-engined all-metal Junkers monoplanes, purchased in the winter of 1920, were built in Germany. The Canadian firm of Imperial Oil Limited bought them through the Junkers agency in New York, and then had them flown across the continent to Edmonton, Alberta.

Two Canadian pilots ferried them to the Alberta capital. One was George Gorman, the other Wilfred "Wop" May, and accompanying them on the long trip was air engineer Peter Derbyshire. The two aircraft reached Edmonton the first week in January, 1921, after a strenuous flight in short stages from New York, and before they were dispatched to a base at Peace River Crossing, several hundred miles north of the city, a brief christening ceremony was held.

The aircraft had already received their Canadian registration, one being G-CADP, the other G-CADQ. The former was given the name of *Vic*, the latter being christened *Rene*. The twin Junkers were to become famous in Canadian history as the first airplanes to penetrate the age-old isolation of the Northwest Territories.

The oil company was anxious to get one of their geologists delivered to Fort Norman in the winter wilderness before the 1921 spring break-up of ice on the Mackenzie River would allow for established summer travel in the north by boat. Plans were

97

to fly geologist W. Waddell to a company oil well situated on Bear Island, downstream a few miles from Fort Norman, and for him to make a number of survey flights in that vicinity.

The company hoped to have the job done, and have him flown back to Edmonton long before the ice break-up, but they overlooked the part nature might play in their otherwise well-laid plans.

Both Junkers were ski-equipped and appeared well suited for the project. For the northern flight Gorman remained pilot of the *Rene* but, as "Wop" May had other commitments, another experienced pilot, Elmer Fullerton, was engaged to fly the *Vic*. An additional engineer, named William Hill, was also signed on.

Adventure was quick in coming. From the base at Peace River the two aircraft carried a fuel supply north on March 22, 1921, establishing a cache at Upper Hay River post, 190 miles from their home airfield. On their return it was discovered that somewhere along the way someone had taken pot shots at them from the ground. The conclusion was reached that maybe it was an Indian, or a white trapper, who had never seen an airplane before. Whoever it was, the shooting was a bit too accurate for comfort. Several bullet holes were found in the metal tail section of the *Vic*, and it was just good luck that a vital part of the machine had not been hit or its occupants injured, with dire results.

When the actual attempt to fly to Fort Norman began on March 24th, the entire north country was still in the ice-bound grip of winter. The journey had been planned with a number of stopovers, the first being Fort Vermilion, where the airmen were welcomed by the excited inhabitants.

On the 25th, 200 miles were added to their logs with a good flight to Lower Hay River post. Deep powdered snow lying to a depth of several feet made landings extremely hazardous and hinting of further difficulties to come. On that date the aerial voyageurs crossed the border of Alberta into the Northwest Territories to become the first men to fly in that section of Canada.

The next day they carried on to Fort Providence, at the western end of Great Slave Lake, encountering several snow storms along the way, which gave them a bad time in the air. After landing, there came a big surprise. Jumping from the cabin door to what they thought was the surface of the snow-covered ground below, they received a decided shock when they plunged into the powdery stuff right up to their armpits.

In a hurry they secured fuel from the Hudson's Bay post supplies and, as soon as that was completed, they endeavoured to take off for Fort Simpson, 165 miles down the Mackenzie River, which was still solidly frozen over from bank to bank. Three times they plowed through the binding snowdrifts before at last they were able to pick up sufficient speed to become airborne. Then off they went, heading north in a beeline for Fort Simpson.

Two hours later they were circling the place, looking for a suitable landing-spot. They had brought along not only geologist Waddell as a passenger, but also Corporal Thorne, a member of the R.C.M.P. who was stationed at Fort Simpson, and at his suggestion Gorman went down to make a landing in a wide space near the post buildings. Scarcely had the skis touched down before there was the crackle of breaking wood. The skis had come in contact with frozen drifts, unseen beneath the smooth surface of the snow. In a great flurry of snow and splinters, the *Rene* was wrenched to a sudden stop, her undergear torn off and the propeller smashed, but no one was injured.

Still circling above, pilot Fullerton witnessed the trouble and, not knowing what had been the cause, he decided to play safe and landed his machine some distance away on a frozen snye of the river. In the vernacular of the north, a snye is a narrow arm of a river or a backwater.

The *Vic's* engine was not operating too smoothly, so it was decided to remove the propeller and landing-gear from that Junkers and to fit them on the *Rene* to put it in good flying condition. This was done and, with only one lap to go to reach Fort Norman, hopes ran high.

With Engineer Hill and geologist Waddell aboard, Gorman endeavoured to make a getaway, but ill-luck still dogged his efforts. Just before they were airborne, and when success seemed within their grasp, the skis struck other hidden drifts and again the undergear was smashed. Worst of all so was the propeller, and they had no spare to take its place.

Long faces were the order of the day when the airmen realized they were going to be marooned at Fort Simpson without any apparent hope of going forward or backward until spring thaws would make it possible to proceed back to Peace River by boat. The blessing of radio communication was not then available in the high north, and winter in that area meant complete isolation from the outside world.

Then a tiny ray of light shone through the gloom enveloping them when someone suggested, "Would it be possible to make new propellers?" Quickly grasping the idea, post manager P. H. Godsell suggested that if it was material that was needed to put the plan over he could help. In the company storehouse were a number of oak and birch planks, primarily intended for use in making sleigh runners. If the airmen wanted to make use of them they were theirs for the asking. Glue to laminate the boards together was also available in the form of a strong adhesive called *babiche*, a French word describing glue made from the hide and hoofs of a moose, a preparation regularly made and used in the north country.

The Catholic Mission near the post, under Father Decoux's guidance, had a splendid workshop, and Walter Johnson, the Hudson's Bay carpenter at the post, was a cabinetmaker by trade and was in possession of a complete set of woodworking tools.

With such an excellent combination of materials and expert asistance at their disposal, the airmen quickly became enthusiastic towards the idea of making new props, and plans were at once discussed to get the job rolling. After two arduous weeks of work gluing the planks together, roughly sawing and chiselling them into shape and finally trimming them up and balancing them, the two home-made propellers were completed. Credit for making them goes fully to William Hill, who had expert knowledge of how they were made, and to Walter Johnson for his knowledge of binding the planks together and his woodworking experience.

Many stories have since been told of that remarkable job and some of the tales have been most inaccurate, some fanciful in the extreme, but all had a basis of truth stemming from the actual facts of that clever feat of making props out of the raw materials the north had to offer.

As the propeller making got under way, the other crew members overhauled the *Vic's* engine, doing the job right out in the open, with temperatures often ranging as low as zero. The ski undergear of both machines were also repaired.

At last the props were completed and fitted to their respective Junkers, and excitement ran high on April 15th when Fullerton test-flew the *Vic*. The home-made prop operated perfectly, without vibration, and when Gorman test-flew the *Rene* on April 20th it seemed their isolation was at an end.

Spring was very close by this time, and it was decided that with ski-equipped airplanes it would be foolish to continue north, to be again marooned there when the spring break-up of ice came and warm winds melted the snow. So plans were made to fly both machines back to their base at Peace River.

Nature does not always co-operate where mere men are concerned. On the night of the 24th an Indian hurried to the post to tell the airmen that the ice on the Mackenzie was beginning to break up.

As both machines were staked out on the ice of a small arm of the river delay in getting away meant they might not be able to do so at all. It certainly did mean that the airplanes would have to be moved immediately or they would be swept away. Before it was daylight on the 25th equipment had been stowed in both aircraft, and the moment it was light enough Gorman attempted a takeoff. It was not his lucky day. The tail section of the all-metal Junkers struck a pothole in the ice before it was airborne, and the resultant damage precluded any chance that craft had of making another attempt.

Using husky dogs and men, the *Rene* was dragged to high ground on the river bank, and Fullerton tried his luck in the *Vic*. All baggage was removed from his machine to lighten it as much as possible, and he planned to fly to a small icebound lake a few miles away where equipment could then be taken and loaded.

Accompanied by Jack Cameron, a local trapper, the airman gave the *Vic* full throttle as the ice began to break up with a tremendous uproar at the other end of the runway. The *Vic* lifted quickly into the air, but as it swept over the maelstrom of ice and churning water the rear tips of both skis trailed along the heaving mass for some distance before they were in the clear. The margin between safety and complete disaster had been mighty narrow. If they had gone down into the grinding, tossing floes nothing could have saved them from complete destruction.

Flying directly to the lake, Fullerton made a good landing, and Cameron led him back to the post through the snow and thick bush. Equipment was then back-packed to the plane from the post, and things were readied for an early departure on the following morning. At 8.00 a.m. on the 26th, Fullerton, Gorman, Hill and Waddell climbed aboard, said farewell to their Fort Simpson hosts and were off, heading for Peace River. Derbyshire remained behind to prepare the *Rene* for repairs when parts could be shipped in by boat.

Things went well for the quartette. The home-made propeller bit smoothly into the northern air, while the rhythmic song of the engine never missed a beat.

After a six-hour flight, covering 500 miles, they arrived nonstop at their Peace River base, and they were just in time. In that lower latitude the spring thaw had set in and there was only just sufficient snow on the ground on which to land. The next day bare patches of ground showed everywhere. It was as close as that.

In a way the first flight into the Northwest Territories was a success in overcoming many obstacles, but it had not served its full purpose so far as Imperial Oil Limited were concerned. There is no doubt, however, that it earned a place of distinction in the exploration history of the north, and it certainly drew attention to the possibilities of air transport in that great area.

Years later the two home-made propellers were acquired by the National Research Council and today they may be seen side by side in a glass case in their Aeronautical Museum at Ottawa. Still in perfect condition, they mark an epic adventure in the north, and remind all who see them that the resourcefulness of our airmen is a heritage of which all Canadians may well be proud.

Part four / ADVENTURE AND ACHIEVEMENT

17. Like a True
Viking Ship

WITH AN ADVENTUROUS CREW aboard, this craft was also a "Viking ship," but not of ancient vintage.

No high carved figurehead adorned its bows, nor did it set forth on its voyages of discovery with white sails filling in the breeze. Instead its bow was streamlined to cleave the air, and it rode the wind on sturdy wings on its journeys afar.

In 1922, one of Canada's earlier flying companies, the Laurentide Air Services of Quebec, decided to procure an amphibian flying-boat for forest patrol and survey and for photographic mapping of their large timber holdings in that Province. Since no airplane of the type they wanted was available for purchase, either in Canada or the United States, an order was placed with the firm of Vickers Limited in England for delivery of one of their Viking five-seater amphibian flying-boats.

The craft reached Canada aboard ship in 1922 and was at once commissioned into use as soon as it was rigged. For many years thereafter it gave splendid service, being used on innumerable missions throughout Canada. On many of those trips it penetrated into far distant wilderness areas, where no airplane had gone before, and few men if any had gone afoot or by canoe.

During its early years it became well known throughout Quebec and Ontario, where it covered thousands of miles in its allotted work. Registered with the lettering G-CAEB, it became better known to foresters and people living in the backwoods as "That EB airplane."

By 1925, its hull had been washed by the waters of Hudson Bay, the St. Lawrence River, Lake Ontario and hundreds of lakes and watercourses located in the eastern provinces.

This same year it was to go much farther afield, to dip its sturdy snout into the clear waters of the Pacific and some of the lakes and rivers of British Columbia and the Yukon.

An American mining syndicate, planning a gold-seeking expedition into the north, decided to make use of an airplane for transporting its men to the area and for moving them about while there. Casting about for a suitable machine, they learned of the Viking owned by the Laurentide people and, after negotiations, hired it for the job on hand, together with two of the company's pilots, J. Scott Williams and Jack Caldwell.

Dismantled and placed aboard a flatcar, the Vickers made the long trip across the continent by train to Prince Rupert, B.C. There the craft was rigged and then flown to Wrangell, Alaska, to pick up a prospecting crew awaiting its arrival.

There were six syndicate men as well as considerable equipment and supplies. This necessitated flying everything in by relays, first to a temporary base far up the Stikine River and then to a permanent base which was established on Dease Lake. It was, and still is, a hunter's as well as a geologist's paradise, but it was forbidding country, hemmed in by immense mountain ranges and far from civilization.

As soon as the main base was set up, parties of two or three mining men were flown to distant locations. They were left there with supplies, to be picked up again at a prearranged date. At that time the entire northern central portion of British Columbia was practically unexplored and unsurveyed, and many of the places the men were flown to were completely inaccessible except by air.

On most of these side trips, the airmen had little idea of their actual whereabouts. Maps they possessed were quite inadequate for positive identification of the terrain. Thousands of square miles showed as only a blank on their maps, and they operated by establishing their own landmarks. Low clouds frequently rolled in over the mountaintops, and without good visibility the airmen were obliged to land on some unknown watercourse if they were caught in such circumstances while in flight. Then they just sat it out and waited for the weather to clear. It was all in their day's work, and a necessary evil if they wanted to play safe and stay alive.

The huge toll of wrecked aircraft which have vanished or been smashed up in that same area during the years since Scott Williams and Caldwell first flew there is ample proof of the dangers lurking there. Today, with all the modern aids and instruments available for safety in flying, the risks to aircraft operating in that wild country in bad weather have not diminished one bit.

"EB" and the party it carried were true flying explorers in every respect, and they spearheaded the use of aircraft in connection with prospecting on the North American continent and probably anywhere else in the world. For six weeks the job went on, until 95 hours' flying time had been logged. That they went far afield from their Dease Lake base can be checked by looking at any good map of the area. On one flight the Viking penetrated 150 miles beyond the northern border of British Columbia, flying into Frances Lake in the Yukon. The astonished manager of the isolated Hudson's Bay post at Fort Frances welcomed them with open arms, being amazed at the new means of transportation—an airplane—which he had never seen before.

When prospecting operations were brought to a close the men were relayed out to Prince Rupert, and the airmen flew on to Vancouver, where the Viking was dismantled and shipped back east. The results of the prospecting venture were never publicly divulged. The syndicate men were very close-mouthed about what they may have found, and if any claims were staked the only people who knew about them were the government officials in the recording office at Victoria.

The Vickers was not to have too long a rest, and in 1926 it again played an important role in another northern flying adventure which took place in the Northwest Territories.

The craft left its original owners for good when it was sold to a group of Calgary businessmen who had formed a company to undertake a gold-seeking venture. They had received a tip relating to a fabulous gold deposit in the northern Barren Lands, and wished to speed up the investigation. Two employees of the Laurentide Air Service were hired as crew of the plane. Pilot Jack Caldwell was one—well recommended as the co-pilot on the previous year's adventure in northern British Columbia—and Irenée Vachon became engineer.

The Vickers went by rail from eastern Canada to Lac la Biche, in northern Alberta, the end of a railway which ran from Edmonton to the shores of the lake from which the village takes its name.

The group called themselves the Northern Syndicate, and it had been formed when a grizzled old prospector had arrived in Calgary, showing a glass jar around jammed to the top with rich-looking gold quartz. When the contents were assayed they proved to be very high in gold content, equalling some of the most productive mines then operating in Canada. It looked like another El Dorado to the men who invested their money in forming the syndicate, especially when the old fellow divulged that his claim was unregistered and was one which required only surface working. The canny old fellow would only give brief hints as to its location. He said that he had left his Indian wife to look after things until he returned, and also mentioned he had set out a large pile of rocks in the form of a rough cross, the better to find his way back.

Once the Viking had been purchased plans moved along quickly, but not quite fast enough to prevent the prospector from getting into real trouble. With some of the first money paid to him for his information he was soon hitting the high spots in the low part of town. One night he became involved in a drunken brawl, and in the ensuing fracas he was struck on the head by a flying bottle and suffered a fractured skull.

Plans had been for him to accompany the air expedition as the number one requirement for locating the spot in the wilderness, where the squaw and the gold awaited his return. Unfortunately, he never came out of his coma and died before any further information could be learned from him.

His passing put the syndicate in a spot. However, they had learned a little from him regarding the general area from which he had come out of the north, so they decided to go ahead with their aerial exploration. The old fellow had dropped hints that the claim was situated north of the Saskatchewan border, beyond the height of land in the Barrens, so they had those vague clues to go on. When the aircraft reached Lac la Biche it was hauled to the lake's edge, where Caldwell and Vachon rigged it for flight right out in the open.

So the Viking ship set off once again on high adventure with gold-seekers aboard, flying first to Fort Fitzgerald and then into the great expanse of the then little known Barrens. It is a vast and rockbound country, dotted with hundreds of thousands of lakes and watercourses of all shapes and sizes. Landmarks of a suitable nature are few and far between, and woe betide anyone afoot or in the air who becomes lost in its huge embrace.

June 30, 1926, found the flying explorers winging away from Fort Fitzgerald, heading into the Barrens and the unknown. Caldwell and Vachon were old hands at bush flying, and on every flight they made in the area it was the latter's duty to continually check their course with the time they had been in the air to make very sure they could always find their way back to base.

Their camp was situated on the height of land which angles across the north of Canada from east to west, and was located at latitude 61° 30′ N., 107° 30′ W. A map of Canada will show the approximate spot. The body of water they camped beside they christened Caldwell Lake, although it does not show as even a pinpoint on any map.

Throughout July and August the search went on, Caldwell and Vachon occasionally flying back to Fort Fitzgerald to obtain supplies and gasoline. Keen eyes scanned the drab terrain below on every flight made, hoping to see a rock-built cross or maybe a puff of smoke rising from a campfire. One or both might well have revealed the location of the mysterious claim, but never a sign did they see. Day after day the search went on, some flights taking the fliers hundreds of miles into the Barrens while others carried them on wide circular sweeps.

A smoky sort of haze on the horizon once raised their hopes, but upon flying nearer it was seen to be a dust cloud rising from the hoofs of a small herd of caribou. The monotonous sameness of the country made it impossible to tell for sure if they had looked over some of it on previous flights, and how near they may have come to spotting the illusive claim is anyone's guess.

Towards the end of August cooler weather set in, and when ice was found one morning on the surface of the lake the hunters knew the time had come to give up the search. If they stayed too long the lake might freeze over completely, and they would be marooned.

Whether the old prospector had played a clever hoax on the syndicate and had raised their hopes with a pack of lies will never be known but the gold in the glass jar he had was not a myth. If his Indian wife had hoped for her husband to return to take her out of that forbidding land then she waited in vain and maybe starvation claimed her, there is no way of telling.

Caldwell eventually flew the group out to Edmonton, and received syndicate orders to carry on with the airplane to the R.C.A.F. Air Station at High River, Alberta, where it went into storage for the winter. When the Viking landed on the runway there at the end of the flight from Edmonton, it added a little more history to its log by becoming the first amphibian airplane ever to make a wheel-landing in Canada.

The Guardian Angel which had looked after "EB's" welfare up to this time apparently decided to take a holiday, and the flying-boat lay in storage at High River for two years, seemingly without anyone caring what became of it.

In 1928 a Calgary resident, Mr. B. Lundy, heard it was for sale and, after purchasing it, had it shipped to Vancouver, B.C., where he had a registered air engineer, William Kading, put it into flying condition.   He had big plans for sending the machine north on a prospecting trip but ill-luck struck the airplane before things got under way.

During a test flight the engine seized up and later inspection proved that the oil which had been used was of inferior quality, quite unfit for such a high-powered motor.   All of the bearings were burnt out, and as the engine appeared to be ruined the Vickers was again put in storage, this time right out in the open, behind a hangar at Vancouver's Airport.

Time passed and, as deterioration set in, its flying days seemed to have come to an end.   Then the Guardian Angel arrived back on the scene in the person of Captain Fred Clarke of Vancouver.   In 1932 he bought the Viking just as it stood and spent a tidy sum putting it back into first-class flying condition.   The engine was stripped down to the last nut and bolt and was completely rebuilt, while all the canvas surfaces were stripped off, to be renewed in the Vancouver plant of Boeing Aircraft, Limited.   When the job was finished a brand-new-looking "EB" stood on the ramp, and the first test flight after its resurrection proved it as airworthy as the day it left the original factory in England.

Clarke, too, possessed the prospecting bug, and intended to launch an air expedition after gold in the spring of 1933.   Things looked rosy and it was a bitter blow for its owner when he learned that it had been destroyed during the final test of the craft before being stored for the winter.

It happened on September 16, 1932.   In charge of pilot Gilbert Jenkins the Vickers was cruising along at about 2,000 feet over the mouth of the Fraser River when the gasoline pipe feeding the carburetor snapped apart.   The fuel flowing through under pressure from a pump sprayed all over the engine and the lower wing, and some of it splashing onto the red-hot exhaust pipes immediately burst into flame.   In a few seconds the entire centre portion of the aircraft was a blazing inferno.

Being treated to a pleasure ride, four friends of Captain Clarke's were aboard as well as the pilot, Gilbert Jenkins.   It was his cool actions which averted what might have resulted in the death of all aboard. Immediately the fire broke out, he pushed the controls forward and went down to the sea in an almost vertical dive. It kept the flames from reaching those aboard, and only when a few feet from the water did he straighten out the blazing craft to make a safe but rough landing on the river. Rescuers in small boats were quickly on the scene, and as the flames engulfed the entire airplane its occupants were snatched from death with only moments to spare.

Shortly after, the charred hull and remnants of the once proud machine sank in shallow water. The Viking went to its Valhalla in fiery glory as the black pall of smoke drifted slowly away to mark its passing. The remains were later dragged up from the river bottom, and although the engine was useless for further operations it was salvaged and presented by Captain Clarke to the National Research Council, who had asked if they might have it.

It was then put into presentable condition and placed in their Aeronautical Museum at Ottawa, where the brief inscription attached to it as it now stands on exhibit reads:

> Napier Lion aircraft engine, No. 24634,
> originally fitted to Vickers Viking aircraft,
> Mark VI, G-CAEB.

That laconic bit of information reveals nothing to visitors who glance at it and the engine, and then pass by. The motor deserves a much better description than that. The people who see it would then be held a little longer to look it over. How interested they would be to learn they were standing before the power plant of a flying-boat which had played such a vital role in Canada's early bush flying history, and what a truly fine "Viking ship" it had been.

18. Air Aid for the
Sealing Ships

DURING A PERIOD of over two hundred years, the hardy sealers of Newfoundland had gradually become steeped in tradition in respect to the methods used for the spotting of the seal herds. To change such a custom needed firm convictions and stout hearts, requirements which Canadian airmen possessed, and they set out to prove it. Flying over the fog-ridden icefields of the North Atlantic, they covered hundreds of square miles over open water in ski-equipped machines. The risks they took were beyond all comprehension, but they were out to make their beliefs stick, and they eventually did.

Sealing far out at sea off the coast of Newfoundland is centuries old, and from its beginning up to very recent years was one of the principal sources of income for the hardy people of the island. The methods of searching out and capturing seals underwent no variation during all that time, and eventually the procedure developed into a tight-bound tradition.

Seals are not as valuable today as they were in the past when their hides and blubber were eagerly sought for and used for many purposes. In the distant past blubber was one of the prime requisites for making tallow candles, which in the era before the use of electric light were an international commodity. The hides were also greatly prized for the fine leather they produced when tanned.

In 1921 two Newfoundland air-pilots, Cotton and Bennett, decided the industry needed modernizing and they considered that airplanes were made for the job. It was their firm contention that locating the main seal herd far out on the Atlantic ice floes would be a task they could fill. In two airplanes they made a wide sweep out over the Atlantic, and were successful in spotting the main herd which consisted of tens of thousands of seals. Unfortunately they were not working in conjunction with the owners of the sealing ships and the knowledge they gained was not put to use.

Very much the same thing happened in March, 1922. The two airmen, on sweeps out over the icefields, again located a vast herd of seals and upon returning to St. John's they at once opened negotiations with the ship-owners to lead their vessels to the area. Several weeks elapsed before terms could be worked out, and by that time the herd and the icefield had drifted out into the Atlantic, and had disappeared.

In 1923 another Newfoundland airman, Roy Grandy, came up with a fresh suggestion. He discussed his plans with Bowring Brothers, who owned several of the larger ships of the sealing fleet. Grandy's idea was for them to procure a suitable small airplane, and to launch into aerial seal spotting themselves. Grandy was an ex-sealing skipper himself, as well as an experienced airman, so it seemed that the plan might turn out to be successful.

Unfortunately, the skippers and crew members of most of the sealing ships were quite hostile towards the use of an airplane, as they still considered that their own ability to find the herds was sufficient. Their forefathers had done it that way for generations, so why change? The ship-owners, well knowing the trend of opinion, were not at all eager to try out airplanes in spite of the fact that they held very favourable thoughts in the matter.

Finally, Grandy prevailed upon Bowring Brothers, to buy a machine, and an 80 h.p. two-seater Baby Avro was purchased in England. It was designed for use with skis, wheels or floats, and was ideal for the job. In due course it was shipped from England to Newfoundland, and an English pilot accompanied it, to be its pilot during the 1923 sealing operations.

A platform was erected on the deck, at the stern of the S.S. *Neptune*, one of the company ships, and the fuselage of the Avro was placed on it, and lashed firmly in place for the trip to the sealing grounds. The wings and tail assembly were stowed below decks. The plan was to rig the craft on reaching the hunting grounds, and then make use of it. Antagonism against the use of an airplane still was widespread, and the Avro was completely ignored.

So another season slipped by and when Grandy learned of the difficulties he arranged with the owners to fly the machine himself the next season. When the fleet moved out of port in March, 1924, the airplane was in attendance as before, but this time it went out on its platform fully rigged. It was also on another vessel, the S.S. *Eagle*, whose skipper was a friend of Grandy's. In this manner the trim little biplane was ready at a minute's notice to be slung overside and put to use. Aboard ship when it sailed Grandy also had along an air engineer named Wallace.

Fortune favoured the airplane at last. When the sealing areas were reached, the animals just didn't seem to exist, and the vast main herd eluded the lookouts at every turn. Being an ex-sealer certainly lent weight to Grandy's request that the airplane be used in an effort to prove its worth.

So, without any enthusiasm from the crew, it was lowered overboard to a suitably large icefield, and after a short runway had been roughly levelled off, the airman climbed into the Avro and took off. With him as an additional observer, went a sailor named Jabez Winsor, apparently one crewman at least who did believe in airplanes. From the air the main herd was soon located, and Grandy estimated it to contain about one hundred and twenty-five thousand seals. The most important factor of the flight was the news that the fleet was cruising away from it.

It was the only flight the airplane made that season, but its value was amply proved. The ships turned about and reached the herd, where they were able to take on capacity catches. That is the way new sealing history was made and a long tradition broken.

In 1925, the Avro acquired a new boss, in the person of pilot Jack Caldwell.

It might be expected that the men of the fleet would have at last welcomed the use of an airplane with open minds, but they certainly did not. When men are steeped in tradition up to their necks their outlook doesn't change easily. The two-seater Avro went out on the *Eagle* as before, but there was much reluctance in making use of it. Fortunately for Caldwell, the age-old hit-and-miss methods of finding the main herd again brought no result.

As the season wore on the airman finally prevailed on the *Eagle's* skipper to put the Avro to work. So it was lowered overside onto an icefield and, with practically no prepared runway for takeoff, Caldwell climbed aboard and set off, flying alone. He was back in ten minutes to tell the captain he had spotted the main herd. Shortly after, he was off again to fly a triangular course of approximately 70 miles, and checked over an area of hundreds of square miles. The information he brought back enabled every ship to again make capacity catches and return to port with full loads in their holds.

The nature of the flying undertaken was extremely dangerous. Fog forms out of nowhere over the icefields, with sudden and unexpected changes in temperature, and when that happens sea and sky quickly become blotted out. If Caldwell had been caught that way when in the air, or his aircraft engine had failed, his chances of survival would have been very small.

At that period, radio had not come into general use in connection with aircraft, and Caldwell possessed no means of keeping in contact with the ship. To aid him in finding the ship on his return, the captain of the *Eagle* issued orders for the ship's furnaces to be well stoked, and the column of black smoke which poured out of the funnel and rose high into the sky proved to be of great assistance to Caldwell in getting back safely.

In March, one of the worst conditions to contend with in that area is a climatic condition which causes sea and sky to merge in the distance, forming just a huge vast void. Without a reliable compass, all sense of direction in the air can quickly be lost—bad business indeed, for an airman, flying over the open sea in a ski-equipped airplane.

During 1926, and in 1927, Caldwell contracted to fly the Avro, going out on both occasions aboard the *Eagle*. It was a comforting experience for him to know that at last all members of the ships were glad to have him along and welcomed his efforts. Numerous flights were made and catches were good, the Bowring vessels always returning to port with full loads.

In between the 1927 and 1928 seasons, Caldwell was given a free hand to select a new airplane for use, and his choice was an Avro Avian, which had a nonstop flying range of five hundred miles.

Elaborate plans were worked out for the 1928 hunt. Land bases for the use of the airplane were selected and established along the coasts of Newfoundland, Labrador, the north shore of the Gulf of the St. Lawrence, and on Anticosti Island in the centre of the gulf itself. At each one caches of 600 gallons of gasoline were placed, together with additional necessary supplies. Aircraft operations then became land based, enabling the pilot to survey far greater areas than ever before.

At the same time serious research began in an effort to learn more about the habits of seals. For hundreds of years they had been hunted, yet very little was known of their migratory existence.

Before a single Bowring vessel left St. John's in 1928 Caldwell made an extensive air sweep of hundreds of miles and, following the advice he brought back, the captains of the ships were able to proceed directly to where the main herd was located. Capacity catches were soon made by all ships and several were able to make port and discharge their hauls and then return to the sealing grounds a second time. That was something which had never happened before in the recorded history of sealing in New-foundland.

It seemed as though airplanes were to become a vital part of the industry, but circumstances changed things in a hurry. Caldwell wasn't available as a pilot in 1929, and an airman named Alex Harvey took over the job. Plans were similar to those of the previous year, but on his first survey flight fog trapped him in the air.　In an emergency landing on the Newfoundland coast the Avian was totally wrecked, although Harvey came out of the mix-up uninjured.

With their aircraft destroyed, and the depression years just beginning to affect business everywhere, the ship-owners decided to quit the use of airplanes, although they had so fully proved their worth.　It is strange how an unwanted aid to the industry proved so successful by finally being fully accepted by the sealers. Then, having won such hard earned recognition, it had to be abandoned on such short notice, and the modern aid to sealing came and went in less than one decade.

So the men of the fleet had to go back to their time-worn hit-and-miss searching, a heritage they had finally learned to dislike, although it had been handed down to them since sealing began off Newfoundland's stormy coast.

19. "Queen of the Yukon"

MANY STORIES WRITTEN about flying in the Canadian north country have built up a fallacy that all bush pilots of the early era were of the devil-may-care type. According to such fictional stuff, few of these airmen had much regard for the safety of their passengers and none at all for their own necks. Nothing could be so utterly false. The companies who pioneered flying in the north employed only the most skilful pilots and equally well trained engineers, all of whom could be relied upon both in the air and on the ground.

Northern conditions required men who could reach their destinations, by dead reckoning if necessary, but always men who possessed common sense. Flying over unmapped terrain, with radio facilities non-existent, called for flight sense of the highest order, even in good weather.

During the pioneer period, when the north was being opened up by air, government subsidy in the form of financial aid to airplane companies just did not exist. Every dollar they earned was won through good organization, coupled with the flying capabilities of their pilots, and the work of their engineers. Difficulties which loomed up all too often were just a part of the job, and they were met and overcome the hard way, simply by trial and error.

The now hackneyed phrase, flying by the seat of their pants, was coined many years before bush flying began, but it caught the fancy of many writers who have written about Canadian airmen. The truth of the phrase, however, is all too true as applied to

121

bush flying. The words actually express the reaction of a pilot when caught in the air in bad flying weather and poor visibility.

It is then that airmen are able to keep their aircraft on an even keel, purely by their physical reaction to the airplane's movements. In simple words, it means the amount, or angle of pressure of the seat against the pilot's rump, which instinctively imparts immediate action of flight controls to maintain a straight or level course. All experienced pilots of the old regime could fly that way but air training today frowns upon such qualifications. The modern method prefers trainees and experienced pilots alike to rely implicitly on their many flying instruments and not on their physical reactions. That is good as applied to modern airplanes but it would not have worked in the early days before so many of the present important aids to flying existed.

When commercial aviation first made its bow in the Yukon, it came with the incorporation of Yukon Airways and Exploration Company Limited, with headquarters at Whitehorse. The firm was organized with private capital of $50,000, and a Ryan monoplane, fitted with a 200 h.p. Wright Whirlwind engine, was selected as a suitable craft for the work ahead. It was a sister ship to the one used by Charles Lindbergh on his nonstop flight from New York to Paris in May, 1927, and no doubt that exploit greatly influenced the choice.

With a part interest in the company, pilot Andrew D. Cruickshank took over the job of flying the machine, his duties also embracing that of manager and engineer. Born in England of Scottish parents, he had served in World War One as a fighter pilot. When it was over he emigrated to Canada and upon arrival enlisted in the R.C.M.P. For the next five years he served with that famous force, on duty mostly in the Yukon. He resigned in 1924 to take up flying again, going to California where he flew for the movies, and later barnstorming throughout the western states, for three years altogether.

Then came the job of flying the Ryan, and to give it a more appropriate name than just the Ryan it was appropriately christened *Queen of the Yukon*. From the San Diego factory where it was built, the craft was flown to Vancouver, B.C., the journey being made in leisurely fashion, as numerous stop-overs at cities were made *en route* to take up paying passengers.

Cruickshank finally reached Vancouver in the Ryan on September 27, 1927, where the machine was dismantled and shipped north aboard the Canadian Pacific S.S. *Princess Mary,* which sailed for Skagway on October 17th. The airman was aboard, and the journey north by boat also became a honeymoon trip. He had married Miss Esmée Bulkley, of Vancouver, the morning the ship was to leave.

On arrival at Skagway on the 21st the monoplane was put ashore and at once assembled. Good facilities for doing so were non-existent, nor was there any suitable area from which the airplane could take off. After looking the place over, Cruickshank had a nearby lumber mill lay planks along a rough road which ran down to the sea. It was a tremendously makeshift runway, but there just was nothing else. It meant that the airman would have but one chance for a getaway, and once in the air he would not be able to return to Skagway except by making a crash landing.

It was incidents such as this that frequently earned for early bush pilots the rating that they were reckless daredevils. Daring they were, but not intentionally foolhardy. It was circumstances similar to those met by Cruickshank that invariably involved them in risky decisions. The airman made very certain that the engine was functioning smoothly at top power before he attempted a takeoff on October 25th. Sharing the risk with him were Clyde Wann, a director of the company, an engineer J. E. Smith, together with Mrs. Cruickshank. Andy did his best to persuade his wife to travel from Skagway to Whitehorse by train, but his pleading fell on deaf ears. Esmée remained firm in her conviction that if he was going to take risks, she was going to be with him when he did, so she went along.

As the *Queen of the Yukon* roared down the rickety runway towards the waterfront, it seemed that it was bound for disaster, but Andy knew what he was doing. He kept the wheels on the planks right up to the last split second. Then as the craft was almost into the sea he yanked back on the controls, and they were in the clear and safely airborne.

Lowering clouds and poor visibility presented a serious menace to safety as Skagway is surrounded by mountainous peaks. As the plane headed north, the airman was obliged to follow a winding course through gullies and along valleys bordered by immense rocky cliffs, until an altitude of 12,000 feet was reached, and at last they were well above the peaks below. Twenty minutes were needed to gain that elevation, and several times rocky bulwarks loomed up out of the mist ahead and only Andy's expert handling of the machine saved them from annihilation.

Going directly over White Pass, they reached Whitehorse at last, an hour and a half after leaving Skagway. The next day they flew on to Dawson, to conclude the maiden flight in the north of the *Queen of the Yukon*.

On November 11, 1927, the inaugural air-mail and passenger service went into effect, connecting the 500 miles of exceedingly rough country between Whitehorse, Dawson and Mayo.

On the initial flight, the entire route was flown nonstop in just under four hours and a half. The contrast with regulation travel in the north at that time proved the airplane's worth. Winter travellers relied on dog-teams to get them from place to place, and to have made the trip from Whitehorse to Mayo in such a manner would have required from twelve to fourteen days of tough going even under good weather conditions.

During the first air-mail flight on November 11th, Mrs. Cruickshank accompanied her husband, and it was her duty to "deliver" the mail bag when they reached Dawson. No stop was scheduled so, when they reached the place, Andy circled very low. Esmée in the meantime had opened a window. As the monoplane swept along just above the main thoroughfare, she pushed the mail sack out through the window, and that was that. It hit the street bang in the middle. It was an unorthodox way of doing it, but it served its purpose that long-ago day when the Yukon received its first delivery of air-mail.

Summer in that area can be quite pleasant for flying, but to go up there and pioneer such work under winter conditions where sub-zero temperatures can be the rule needed great determination and courage.

As flying went on that winter, Mrs. Cruickshank accompanied her husband on the majority of trips he made, often when ground temperature was forty below. What it was in the air is anyone's guess. The radial Wright engine was well suited to that climatic condition. It was air-cooled but, considering the Ryan did not possess ski landing-gear but only wheels, Andy's prowess as a pilot can well be understood.

All of the mail flown the first two years of operation was carried under permission of the Dominion of Canada postal authorities. Other than that official blessing the government lent no further aid, either financially or with publicity. The air-mail carried by Yukon Airways and Exploration was strictly their own business, whether it flourished or not. On top of regulation postal rates on each item of mail flown, the company was allowed to assess an extra carrying charge of twenty-five cents per letter and proportionally more for parcels. The sum was collected from the sender at the point of mailing, and the company issued their own designed "stickers" for affixing to all mail flown.

Envelopes carried on the initial first flight on November 11, 1927, are valued in stamp catalogues today at approximately $40.00 each. If signed by Andy Cruickshank, they are worth $5.00 more.

In 1928 Andy left the services of the company to accept a pilot's position with Western Canada Airways and, several months after he had left, the *Queen of the Yukon* was wrecked at Mayo, killing its pilot, Cameron, who was the sole occupant. The flight had been planned as the first one to connect the Yukon with Aklavik, at the mouth of the Mackenzie River in the Northwest Territories. The smash-up took place when the airman was landing on a lake at Mayo, and the craft plunged through the surface to become a shattered wreck, and the *Queen of the Yukon* was a queen no more.

20. Winter Wings of Mercy

THE INDIAN, LOUIS BOURASSA, with his sleigh and team of husky dogs, slowly diminished with the distance until their rhythmic movement merged into black dots, to finally vanish in the snow-white waste of the frozen river. Far behind him the small group of residents at Little Red River watched with fear and anxiety in their hearts as the man and his team disappeared from their sight.

Some three hundred miles south was the nearest telegraph office. It was the Indian's responsibility to trek out over the winter wilderness to reach Peace River town, carrying news to be sent to Edmonton. It was bad news and he must waste no time on the trail. The health authorities at Edmonton had to be informed as quickly as possible that the dread disease of diphtheria was rampant at Little Red River and that they were in dire need of help.

Mr. Logan, a Hudson's Bay Company employee at the post, had already died from the malady and many others were showing symptoms of being inflicted.

Doctor H. A. Hammon, the only physician for hundreds of square miles around, had a small amount of serum available for treating diphtheria but it was not fresh. He was greatly afraid that the disease might spread to tragic epidemic proportions if outside help could not be obtained.

In the hope that such assistance could reach them in time to avert such a catastrophe, the Indian musher had been entrusted with the responsibility of trekking to railhead at Peace River to send off the vital telegram to the Minister of the Board of Health at Edmonton, giving him details and requesting immediate aid. During Bourassa's heroic and exhausting trek the temperature stood far below zero. Covering the rough winter trail at break-neck speed, both man and dogs suffered severely under such bitter conditions during the fourteen days they were on the trail.

The journey began on December 18, 1928, but it was not until January 1, 1929, that the weary man and his exhausted team finally staggered into Peace River and the vital message was dispatched to Edmonton.

Once the news reached there the predicament of the people of Little Red River quickly became news. As the health officials cast about for a quick method of delivering the sorely needed medical supplies, they contacted an Edmonton flying company and the news became headlines.

At that time, two partners named Vick Horner, and Wilfred "Wop" May, were operating a small flying company at Edmonton, named Commercial Airways of Alberta, Limited. They owned one small airplane, a two-seater open-cockpit, Avro Avian biplane, powered with an air-cooled 75 h.p. engine. Both airmen were World War One pilots, and when asked if they could tackle the job of flying to Little Red River, 600 miles to the north, they at once accepted the challenge—this in spite of the fact that their small airplane possessed only wheel landing-gear, and no skis were then available to replace them for the flight into the snow-covered wilderness.

The Board of Health procured sufficient diphtheria antitoxin to treat 200 cases, together with a number of special surgical instruments frequently required in the treatment of the disease. Outdoor temperatures were well below zero at the time, so the precious toxin was packed in thick wrappings of blankets, with a charcoal-burner inside to keep the contents warm enough to prevent possible freezing, which would have rendered the serum useless.

Just after noon on January 2nd, less than twenty-four hours

after the vital message had been received from Peace River, Horner and May climbed into the Avian and, with the antitoxin stowed aboard, they set out on their flight of mercy.

Three hours later, and 265 miles north of Edmonton, early darkness in that latitude forced them to stop, and they landed at the tiny community of McLennan Junction. All the way from Edmonton, the airmen had been obliged to fly at a very low height to keep in visual contact with the ground and the railway track going north. Visibility from the plane was so bad that much of the time they flew at less than a hundred feet above the ground to prevent getting lost.

Midwinter morning daylight is late in coming in the north, and it was impossible for them to get away from McLennan Junction until 9.40 a.m. on the 3rd. Then they were off, heading for Peace River where they stopped only briefly to refuel. From then on they were strictly on their own as they left the comforting tracks of the railway behind and headed out over the wilderness.

Through the gloom of that sub-zero day they set out for Fort Vermilion, following along the frozen course of the Peace River, and they made the 280 miles to that Hudson's Bay post by 4.30 p.m. Badgered by snow storms and the bitter cold all the way, they arrived as night was falling and the few people there had no idea of their coming.

They could not fly at night and, as dawn was many hours away, the precious serum was placed snugly aboard a sleigh and a musher with his team trekked through the darkness to deliver the toxin to the anxious doctor, who still awaited word as to whether the message for help had reached Edmonton or not. The entire number of residents of Little Red River soon received inoculation and the spread of the disease was brought to a halt, happily, without further loss of life.

With their job completed, the two airmen left Fort Vermilion to return south on the 4th, and reached Peace River in the afternoon. Temperatures had dropped severely and stood at 33 degrees below zero as they continued south, cold flying weather for men seated in open cockpits. When the Avian rolled to a stop at Peace River, both airmen were so numbed with cold they had to be assisted from the machine, and both had suffered from frostbite.

January 6th saw their triumphant return to Edmonton, where great enthusiasm prevailed. Their families, members of the press and a huge crowd of people were on hand to greet them and congratulate them on their fine achievement. By this time their exploit had become world news.

The fact that the serum reached Little Red River in time to avert a possible epidemic was a feather in the cap for the Edmonton Board of Health, but the credit was only theirs in part. The real glory went to four stout-hearted men, two Indian mushers and two daring airmen, together with two sturdy teams of husky dogs, who unknowingly played their vital part in the success of the entire affair.

21. The Sturdy Moths

THIS IS NOT A STORY concerning a single aircraft, but one which tells of a large number of airplanes, the Gipsy Moths and the Tiger Moths, built by the De Havilland Aircraft Company of Canada. Both types were two-seaters, and they played a tremendous part in Canada's forward progress in the training of men and women to fly.

Judged by airplanes of most modern standards the Moths were tiny craft, but within their strong built nose reposed a Cirrus air-cooled engine which in its day was just about the most reliable airplane motor found anywhere in the world.

The first of the two types to go into use in Canada was the Gipsy Moth, sixty of which had been built in England and then shipped out to the company's small factory at Toronto, where they were assembled and test flown.

Light two-seater airplanes were in great demand in Canada in 1928, particularly for student training, and after the original group of sixty Moths had been shipped from England plans were quickly formed to have all additional demands filled by having the Moths built in Canada. The need arose with the establishment of many flying clubs throughout Canada under the sponsorship of the Dominion government. Of numerous airplanes available, the dainty Gipsy was selected for the work ahead, and became generally adopted for use with the various flying organizations.

The Royal Canadian Air Force, realizing the adaptability of

the machine for many purposes, wisely selected it, using it for student elementary training and on various types of service undertakings.

The De Havilland Tiger Moth was a later model of very similar design to the staunch Gipsies but possessing additional improvements, one being an engine of more horsepower. The Tiger Moth quickly came into its own with the outbreak of World War Two, when it was adopted by the Royal Canadian Air Force as its standard elementary training plane under the Commonwealth Air Training Plan. Shortly after the war broke out it was realized that the demand for trained airmen must go forward with greater speed. To accomplish this, young men from all parts of the British Commonwealth were enlisted and sent to Canada to undergo training under the Commonwealth Air Training Plan. Tens of thousands of keen young fellows thus received their initiation in the air flying a Tiger Moth.

A total of 1,747 Tiger Moths were built specially for elementary flying training purposes, and practically every student who learned to fly in Canada during the years of World War Two received some initial training in a Tiger Moth.

During peacetime a considerable number of interesting flights took place in Canada directly attributable to the use of a Gipsy, especially between the years of 1927 and 1939.

The first airplane ever to fly in the "high north" in Canada, in the northeastern area, not far south of the Arctic Circle, was a two-seater Gipsy Moth seaplane. It had been taken north with six other larger aircraft and equipment when the Hudson Strait Expedition went into the Hudson Strait area in 1927 for the purpose of a year's survey. The object of the expedition was to record, and photograph daily ice conditions and gather information along the strait which connects Hudson Bay with the Atlantic Ocean. On arrival at Port Burwell, on the south shore at the entrance to Hudson Strait, the Gipsy was put overside from the ship, and became the first Canadian airplane flown in that northern area, when it was piloted by Squadron Leader T. A. Lawrence, and Flight Lieutenant A. A. Leitch.

The flight, made on July 27, 1927, was the first of a great many done by the other machines. The Gipsy's use was confined to searching out suitable locations at which permanent bases could be established for the work ahead, of which three were later set up. One was at Burwell, another at Wakeham Bay, halfway along the south shore of the Strait, and the third was on Nottingham Island at the entrance to Hudson Bay. A storm later destroyed the small Gipsy Moth, but by then it had fully served the purpose it had been sent to perform in adding to Canadian flying achievement.

Another Gipsy Moth was flown across Canada on two separate occasions and back again, the pilot being Sir James MacBrien, then president of the Canadian Flying Clubs. His object in making the flights was to stimulate flying interest in Canadians with a view to gaining more members for the clubs. Up to June 30, 1931, the airman had flown the Moth more than 50,000 miles, and never once did it falter.

Some of Canada's most famous flying personnel, who now hold key positions in the industry, made their first solo flights in a Moth. Many of them spent their entire training hours in one of the versatile two-seaters during the time they were aloft as students in the cockpit of a sturdy Moth.

22. Early Aerial
Workhorses

DURING THE LATE 1920's and continuing through the 1930's, Fairchild and Fokker aircraft, singly or teaming together, were the means by which the Canadian northland was fully opened up by air. The men who flew them were a breed apart, and the wonderful tradition they have left behind them has earned for them world-wide recognition as Canada's famous bush pilots.

To persons unacquainted with the north and the rough wilderness it is composed of, the word "bush" may well be misunderstood. It can easily give the impression that the country it refers to is covered with low bushy vegetation. Nothing could be more inaccurate.

Bush, in Canadian lore, means anything relating to the wilderness. The word covers the vast forested areas of Quebec and Ontario, the bleak rock-bound land of Labrador and the great northern Barren Lands themselves. It is applied to the hundreds of thousands of square miles of the Northwest Territories, with its almost limitless lakes, muskegs and waterways. The entire isolated fastness and rugged terrain of the Rocky Mountains is encompassed under the word "bush," and so is the huge area of the Yukon. It can well be understood therefore that the aircraft and the pilots who penetrated such areas during the pioneer northern flying era were indeed planes and men of high calibre and stamina.

Although flying of a type swept Canada after the end of World War One, much of it for a few years consisted of brief passenger hops or stunt flying, but it did lead the way for the commercial exploits which were soon to follow.

Various types of airplanes used during the war were more or less converted to commercial use in Canada during the first few years of the 1920's, and although some served quite well other types adopted proved to be almost useless. With many such airplanes pilots were loath to venture beyond the fringes of the vast northland.

Then in the late 1920's along came the Fokkers and the Fairchilds, so well able to fly farther afield. The government and commercial firms alike soon put them into service, and the conquering of the high north by air began.

The first five Fairchild FC2's assembled in Canada, were rigged at the Vickers plant at Montreal in 1927. The next year the same firm undertook the building of Fokker Universals, so the two truly fine aircraft grew up together. They were both ideal aerial workhorses, and no sooner were they in service than far horizons in the northland became their objective, and the sound of throbbing aircraft engines was heard in many distant parts of the wilderness for the first time.

From the beginning of 1927, Fokkers and Fairchilds penetrated farther and farther afield on missions of varying descriptions, and the Canadian government, realizing the worth of both types of aircraft, were quick to put some of them into service on various projects, the first being in connection with air-mail routes in eastern Canada.

The sum of $75,000 was set aside by the Federal government to test and establish the possibilities of air-mail operations between Rimouski, on the lower St. Lawrence River, and the City of Montreal.

First flights were inaugurated in September, 1927, when incoming and outgoing Atlantic liners were met, and mail was transferred from or to them, greatly speeding up delivery of first-class postal matter between Great Britain and Canada. In October the route was lengthened to reach Ottawa, and a

Fairchild seaplane, piloted by H. N. Pasmore, became the first aircraft to carry a load of overseas mail from Rimouski to the nation's capital.

Another government-established air-mail route which began in 1927 was one of winter operation, carried out between Murray Bay and Seven Island, along the northern shore of the St. Lawrence River. Canadian Transcontinental Airways were awarded the job, and they purchased a ski-equipped Fairchild in New York. Pilot Romeo Vachon flew the craft from the factory to Murray Bay. As he flew over the City of Quebec *en route*, he threw out a bag of mail at the nearby airport. The bag was attached to a parachute, the first delivery of that type to take place in Canada. Every one of the envelopes which floated down that day are now worth $30.00 each.

Yet another government-sponsored winter air-mail project started in 1927, bringing real drama into the lives of the hardy residents on the Magdalen Islands in the Gulf of the St. Lawrence. Due to the icy conditions on the ocean during the winter months the islands were practically isolated from the mainland, and people living there rarely received or sent out mail during that period. There was a happy celebration when the first airplane reached the Islands on January 11, 1928. It, too, was a Fairchild seaplane, flown by pilot J. Cooper, who had come to them from Moncton, New Brunswick. His engineer was H. W. Francis.

Landing conditions were completely different at each end of the route. Although Cooper was using a pontoon-equipped plane, he was obliged to fit ski runners beneath the float for use on the snow-covered runway at Moncton. He never knew until he arrived over the Magdalens whether ice floes would prevent water landings. When that happened, he was obliged to land on an ice-bound lake on Grindstone Island, and so another unique development for combined landings on either water, snow or ice came into effect for the first time anywhere in the world.

While the Fairchilds were making a name for themselves in Canada the Fokkers were not idle. The Canadian government chose six of them for a twelve-month project which involved aerial survey of the Hudson Strait, the wide stretch of seaway which connects the North Atlantic with Hudson Bay. Adapted for use with either skis or pontoons, the Fokkers were flown almost daily, summer and winter, during 1927-1928, whenever conditions allowed.

Throughout the year's operations one plane was lost. It was forced down on Atlantic icefields, miles off shore from the Labrador coast, when fuel ran out after the pilot had become lost. Only the fact that an Eskimo observer was with them saved the lives of the two airmen in the plane. The native knew how to live off the country and how to survive under such conditions. Even so, the three men were able to hike back to their base only with the greatest difficulty, after trekking for twelve hazardous days over the ice floes and the desolate Labrador terrain. The abandoned Fokker was never seen again.

In conjunction with earlier plans for the selection of a port site on Hudson Bay, which would serve a shipping route up the Bay and along Hudson Strait to the Atlantic, a fine air exploit took place in March, 1927. It was performed by two pilots of Western Canada Airways, Fred Stevenson and Bernt Balchen. They had the job of flying from railhead in Manitoba to Churchill on Hudson Bay, carrying a number of surveyors and engineers upon whose findings rested the final selection of Churchill as the terminal port which marks the northern end of the present Hudson Bay Railway.

The flying job had to be done in a hurry, as it was the tail end of winter when the work began. Flying in some of the toughest winter flying conditions which could be experienced, the airmen transported the men and materials to Churchill, and the survey job was then conducted without a hitch. The port is today one of the busiest spots in the north, and huge shipments of grain now go there by rail, to be loaded into ships which ply back and forth from European ports during the ice-free summer months.

One experience suffered by pilot Stevenson during the flying operations between Churchill and railhead had humorous implications, but it was not funny for him. Flying alone, on the way back from Churchill on one trip, an engine oil pipe broke and he was obliged to land on a small snow-covered lake in the wilderness, seventy-five miles short of base. Unable to repair the trouble without suitable materials, Stevenson sat it out in the cabin the first night, with the wolves howling dismally all around. The next day he set out to walk back to base, realizing his friends had no idea where he was.

He was fortunate to come across a cabin, and to find its Indian trapper-owner at home. Stevenson soon arranged with the man to guide him out, and they set off to slug through the snow-covered bush with food and other items on a sleigh drawn by several half-starved dogs.

In the meantime, the group at railhead had flown out to look for him and had discovered the downed plane, but no pilot. He had left a note in the cabin, telling of the engine trouble, and also of his walking out. As they had no idea where he was, the engine was repaired, and the Fokker was then flown back to base.

Three days later, frostbitten and weary, Stevenson and the guide emerged from the bush, and the first thing the airman saw staring him in the face was the machine he had abandoned on the distant lake. His heartfelt adjectives were luridly spontaneous. With seventy-five strenuous miles behind him on foot, when he could have flown out if he had waited, who can blame him for "blowing his top."

By 1928, numerous commercial flying companies realized the value of the Fairchilds and the Fokkers for northern operations and they were quick to buy them. Both types of aircraft were equally popular. During 1928 twenty-eight Fairchilds were registered for use in Canada, and exactly the same number of Fokkers.

Western Canada Airways set the ball rolling so far as civil companies were concerned when they placed orders for Fairchilds for use in Ontario carrying passengers, mail and freight to the then newly-discovered Red Lake gold area. Flying in the north on a commercial basis was at last on the move, and the next two years saw a phenomenal growth of such flying in all directions, the brunt of the work being handled equally by Fairchilds and Fokkers.

Accomplishments followed quickly on the heels of each other as bush pilots hit their stride. Fuel caches were established at points which penetrated farther and farther into the north until a great network of aerial routes began to form, which finally encompassed the entire country far beyond the Arctic rim.

On September 3, 1928, the fastness of the Canadian Barren Lands bowed to final defeat, when pilot "Punch" Dickins flew a Western Canada Airways Fokker 850 miles nonstop across its eastern spread, flying from Baker Lake in the north, south to Stony Rapids. His engineer was Bill Nadin, and the flight was chartered by mining men C. D. H. MacAlpine and Richard Pearce.

Then it fell to a Fairchild to snatch a little extra glory, when Squadron Leader Earl Godfrey and Sergeant Major Graham, of the Royal Canadian Air Force, made a trans-Canada flight which began on September 5, 1928. They made the flight in an elapsed time of three days, over five long laps. The official mail they carried from Ottawa to Vancouver also made history as the first to be flown across Canada by seaplane.

Then came a teaming-up job by the two famous "F's", when the first winter penetration of Hudson Bay on a commercial venture took place. Each machine was ski-equipped, and they were owned by Northern Aerial Minerals Exploration Company, a name which at once stirs the imagination to think of adventure both in the air and on the ground.

The pilots were instructed to fly to Richmond Gulf from a base in southern Ontario, their job being to pick up a stranded survey crew which winter had caught in its grip.

A blizzard enveloped both airplanes when they were flying north well out over the frozen reaches of Hudson Bay. Together they landed on the ice, and for three days in the semi-darkness of the storm the crews sat in the machines, waiting patiently for a break. With pilots "Doc" Oaks and Pat Reid were two engineers, Murray and Mews. Two passengers also suffered with them on the cold wait, a minister and his bride, whom the airmen had been entrusted to deliver to the Mission at Rupert House, well up the frozen east coast of Hudson Bay.

Finally the storm blew itself out, and off they flew. The newlyweds reached their wilderness home safely, and the waiting survey men were picked up and flown out to Cochrane, Ontario. A cheerless but successful adventure, it marked the beginning of commercial flying in the north in winter.

It was the lot of two ski-equipped Fairchilds to be the first airplanes to penetrate the really high north under winter conditions. The project was organized by Dominion Explorers, owners of both machines. The purpose of the flight was to visit mining bases at a time of year when it would have been practically impossible to do so by ordinary means of travel. It took place beginning in mid-March, a month which may not seem one to offer much trouble to aircraft, if thoughts are allowed to centre on flying in southern areas. However, really tough climatic conditions still exist in March up north, where the winter hangs on until well into May.

The two airplanes flew out of Winnipeg heading for Baker Lake, situated at the eastern end of the Northwest Territories and well up towards the top of the west coast of Hudson Bay. They experienced plenty of trouble and tough climatic conditions before they were flown out again, after covering more than 5,000 air miles on their adventure.

One thing learned was that after making a landing in zero temperatures it was essential to drain the oil from the engine sump while it was still hot. If oil was left in the motor until it cooled it congealed solid, and many hours of work then had to be done, heating up the motor with blowtorches before it could again be started. Another thing found out was that immediately after landing on snow or ice it was necessary to place pieces of wood or something similar under the skis to raise them off the snow. If that was not done the skis froze solid to the ground and then had to be tediously chopped free with an axe.

Stan McMillan and Charles Sutton were pilots in charge of the two Fairchilds, and the latter airman had with him a newly-developed sun compass, invented by Mr. Albert H. Bumstead, of the National Geographic Society. The instrument proved of immense aid to navigation in the area where they were flying.

Landmarks were new to the pilots and the magnetic compass was, and still is, erratic and completely unreliable in that part of the world.

Other significant flights which helped to open the north came in rapid sequence. The Arctic Circle was crossed by airplane in Canada for the first time on July 1, 1929. Great excitement prevailed at Aklavik, at the mouth of the Mackenzie River, when pilot "Punch" Dickins came winging in from the south and landed his Fokker monoplane just offshore.

To seemingly keep the balance equal, a Fairchild was the first to cross the "Circle" in eastern Canada. On August 25, 1929, the machine, under pilot Sutton, landed at the northwest tip of Hudson Bay. He had with him a mining engineer and his own mechanic, the former having been sent to Repulse Bay to check up on some mineral deposits in that area. During one flight Sutton flew north across the Arctic Circle on a route which carried him over Committee Bay, and the penetration of the Arctic at both ends of Canada was finally accomplished.

To meet the ever-growing demand for more airplanes for flying over the "bush," Fairchild Aircraft Limited built a large factory on the outskirts of Montreal and, beginning in 1929, production of their machines was carried on in Canada. The next year the prairie air-mail routes were established, Western Canada Airways contracting to do the job for the Dominion government. The routes linked the major cities of Alberta, Saskatchewan and Manitoba together, and daily air-mail between them proved a great boon. Fairchilds and Fokkers carried on the brunt of the work, along routes flown by night as well as by day, until the depression came along and the entire project was discontinued in 1932.

The two famous "F" aircraft dominated bush flying for many years but other manufacturers, sensing the good market for their products, were not long in getting some of their machines into use, but by that time most of the northern air routes had been pioneered.

Photography, forestry patrol and survey by air developed into routine jobs, and government officials, miners, trappers and businessmen alike, soon were being flown to far-distant points in the north. Freight and air-mail played a major role in financing early flying of this nature, as government mail contracts helped to bolster flying companies' assets.

When the first search and rescue by air took place in the northern British Columbia-Yukon area in 1930, a single Fairchild aircraft, named the *Claire*, bore the entire responsibility. It operated during bitter winter conditions and over country which still makes a pilot shudder to look at it if his thoughts dwell on engine failure in such a mountainous area.

The machine was owned by the Tredwell Yukon Company, of Whitehorse, and flown by an American airman, Everett Wasson. The search was conducted for three people lost along the upper reaches of the Liard River, in then unmapped and tremendously rugged terrain.

For six weeks, from October until well into December, Wasson, together with a northern guide, Joe Walsh, scoured the wilds from the air, doing so under daily conditions of storm and driving snow.

At last they located two of the stranded men but the pilot of the downed Junkers aircraft, in which they had been passengers, had already died from privation and lack of food.

Engine failure or one single error of judgment during the search would have meant almost certain death for Wasson and Walsh, and then the two they rescued would never have been found.

In recognition of their heroism the Canadian and British Columbia governments combined in presenting a $1,500 gift to Wasson and one of $500 to Walsh. It was an epic rescue in northern bush-flying annals which has not been surpassed to this day.

Throughout the 1930's Canada's military air strength was bolstered by the use of many Fairchilds and Fokkers, the R.C.A.F. making very good use of them on aerial photography and forestry patrols in all parts of the country.

Time has passed and with the years the two famous types gradually faded from the flying picture, old age wielding the club which brought them down. No more are their familiar wings seen in our northern skies, and as they were gradually withdrawn a newer look in airplanes took over.

Larger aircraft of varying types and of greater carrying capacity and flying range came into use, carrying on where the Fairchilds and Fokkers left off.

These larger craft have also left their mark on our aerial progress, and the work still goes on unabated as the big machines ply their many routes under the now familiar axiom of the flying boxcars.

23. Flying Boxcars
—Past and Present

"FLYING BOXCARS" is a phrase which was coined years ago. The two words helped to explain the work big airplanes were doing in the air similar to the carrying capacities of railway boxcars on the ground.

As far back as October, 1931, the firm of Canadian Airways Limited purchased a huge German-built Junkers all-metal monoplane, and it was first commissioned for use operating from a base on the Red River at Winnipeg. It was registered under the lettering CF-ARM, and in the years which followed it became a familiar sight at many far-flung points in the northland.

Adaptable to floats, wheels or skis, as climatic or geographical conditions demanded, it was a versatile craft and ideally suited for heavy cargo hauling by air. It was one of the biggest air freighters in its day, weighing four and a half tons empty. Even so, it was still capable of lifting two tons of extra weight, and could then fly a distance of one thousand miles nonstop.

It is quite easy to understand with such capabilities, why it so quickly earned the name of "The Flying Boxcar." A very wide door on either side of its fuselage allowed for extra bulky cargo items to be moved inside. Another large door, or hatch, was built into the top of the fuselage and very heavy pieces of freight could be lowered by a crane into the craft's roomy interior. Metal eyebolts and rings, firmly attached to the inside of the fuselage at strategic points, enabled handlers to lash all goods firmly in place to prevent cargo movement while in the air.

After five years of continuous service, summer and winter, the original 600 h.p. German-built engine was replaced with a British-built Rolls-Royce "Buzzard" motor of still greater horse power. The flying performance was thus increased to a higher degree.

"Old Farm," as it was generally referred to, was the original "flying boxcar" to be put into use in the western hemisphere, and the name so much heard today stemmed from that craft, the granddaddy of them all.

Many of the biggest mining and constructional jobs in the north during "Old Farm's" flying existence can give full credit to their initial start through the efforts of the big Junkers and its pilots in flying essential workmen and materials to designated spots.

On one massive undertaking, it was used to fly in a total of 500 tons of miscellaneous freight and many men to establish a complete mining operation at Cassumit Lake, Ontario. Each flight to the mine site, and return to railhead, required only a 150-mile journey, but the catch was that it was over otherwise completely impenetrable muskeg country where ground travel could only be made during freeze-up.

When the huge Manouan Lake Dam project was constructed in eastern Canada, the Junkers contributed tremendously towards the early success of the undertaking. It flew in all the heavy and bulky machinery and equipment which smaller airplanes could not begin to handle.

Such items as bulldozers, tractors, a twenty-foot motorboat and teams of horses and oxen went into "Farm's" big interior on successive flights over the 110-mile trip from the nearest supply point to the construction site in the wilderness. The biggest item of all was an immensely heavy diesel-powered shovel, the bucket of it alone weighing 4,000 pounds. Of course the apparatus was dismantled as much as possible to facilitate its carriage by air. Some extra large parts had to be cut up by acetylene torch to be transported, and then were welded together again on arrival at the site of the dam.

At still another huge construction project, the Shipshaw Aluminum plant in Ontario, "Farm" handled the major portion, flying in some 4,000 tons of freight load by load.

From such a splendid beginning in hauling freight by air, work of this nature has now spread to all parts of Canada and has become a stabilized part of the nation's economy.

Larger and much more powerful air giants now ply our airways on a network of routes which serve, or can be chartered to serve, every part of the country.

One of the latest of these modern flying freighters is the Fairchild "Packet," known to the industry as the C-119. Many of these twin-engined monsters have been commissioned for use by the Royal Canadian Air Force and commercial flying companies, and they, too, soon received the nickname of "flying boxcars" to carry on a famous tradition. Big as the Junkers was in its day, compared with the more modern "Packet" it seems a small craft today.

The big Fairchild's twin-engines develop a total of 7,000 h.p. between them compared with the original flying boxcar's 600 h.p. Then again, each "Packet" is capable of lifting a 7-ton payload, and with that huge weight in its hold it can set off and fly 3,480 miles nonstop at a cruising speed of 296 miles per hour.

These mighty, distant relatives of the staunch old Junkers, have been in much demand by the R.C.A.F., and did yeoman work flying every required commodity into the northern areas during the construction of the chain of radar warning stations now established up there.

Air freighting has come to stay and has spread to all parts of the world, and many airline officials are quite outspoken in their belief that as the years pass such transportation will equal if not surpass the railroads in the carrying of certain types of commodities.

Looking back at the valued service "Farm" gave, and the immense progress in such work since, there is no reason why we should doubt the experts with their progressive plans for the future.

Part
five /   ATLANTIC SAGA

24. Junkers Journey

ON APRIL 13, 1928, electrifying news hit the headlines all over the world, big print emblazoning the fact that the North Atlantic had finally been flown nonstop the hard way. That meant a plane and its crew had at last conquered the ocean flying in a westerly direction, a feat never accomplished before. Numerous other fliers had attempted it but all had failed, some of them losing their lives in the effort.

The reason why flying from east to west was such a risky business was the strong winds which prevail and sweep endlessly across the North Atlantic in a direction from west to east. The consequent head resistance tremendously cuts down an aircraft's forward air speed, to greatly increase the elapsed flying time required to make it across.

Then at last, it was done.

In a wheel-equipped all-metal Junkers monoplane, the *Bremen*, three courageous men had set off from an airfield on the outskirts of Dublin, Ireland, with the avowed intention and high hope of flying all the way to New York nonstop. The trio was composed of an Irishman, Major Fitzmaurice, and two Germans, Baron von Huenefeld and Captain Koehl.

From the moment they left Ireland behind until their flight concluded in a flurry of swirling dirt, shattered pieces of under-gear and a splintered propeller, it was a completely exhausting trip. Terrific weather plagued them all the time as they drove forward into the rough gale-force winds. No one man could ever have stuck it out at the controls during the thirty-seven hours it took them to make it across.

149

The cockpit in which the pilot sat was wide open to wind and weather, with only a small windshield in front of his face to afford some protection. The fuselage was of cabin design and as one man flew the other two rested inside, gaining what small comfort they could in its cold and pitching interior.

No attempt at actual navigation was made. They flew by compass bearing or by dead reckoning, as they saw fit. They had no other means of keeping to a course, and it proved to be a method almost worse than useless. The incessant strong winds carried them far off course but they had no idea how much until the flight was over.

All through the night of the 12th they slugged it out, nature seemingly dead set against them every minute.

At long last, the greying dawn caught up with them from the east, but they were still far out over the ocean. As the day wore on into afternoon, the airmen peered anxiously ahead, hoping to catch a glimpse of land—any land, because they were worried, thinking perhaps they were so far off course to the north they might well be heading into northern open water and complete annihilation.

As their eyes searched through the storm, an indistinct, vertical object, loomed through the haze below. At first, they believed it to be the funnel of a ship and it was a welcome sight, but it proved to be more so seconds later when it was seen to be the tower of a lighthouse. Their relief was immense, when they realized land of some nature lay below, although where its location was they did not know.

The fuel gauge showed clearly enough that they could not carry on much longer, and in their own exhausted condition, they knew they were even nearer the failure point than was their engine. The decision was made at once to try for a landing, and they began circling about in the vicinity of the lighthouse, in an endeavour to locate a suitable spot. Rain and haze was now their biggest enemy but at last through poor visibility a fair-sized area seemed to serve.

Just as Alcock and Brown were misled when they landed on an Irish bog after their flight across in 1919 from Newfoundland, the *Bremen's* crew suffered the same illusion.

They were tired almost beyond further endurance and anxious to bring the flight to a conclusion without delay. Flying and landing judgment at such times is invariably at a low ebb. Many of the long-distance flights in the early years ended up in crack-ups, and the *Bremen's* arrival in the New World was no exception.

Almost as soon as the wheels of the craft had touched down, large boulders scattered about the area were a quick match for them and the undergear was wrenched away. On its metal belly the *Bremen* quickly slewed to a stop, but not before the prop had vanished in a mass of flying splinters.

The lighthouse keepers were the first persons to reach and greet the airmen as they staggered out of the machine, cold and weary, to jump down to the very welcome ground on which they had so roughly arrived.

It was then that they received a real surprise, when they learned they were so many hundreds of miles off course. They were not in the United States or Newfoundland, nor even in Canada, but they had been lucky. They learned they were on Greenly Island, situated between Newfoundland and Labrador, in the Strait of Belle Isle.

The lightkeepers experienced as much astonishment as the airmen, when they in turn learned the trio were arrivals from a nonstop flight from Ireland. The radio at the lighthouse soon had the news of the landing speeding out over the airwaves, and the world then learned the airmen were safe, and that the east-to-west nonstop crossing of the North Atlantic had been negotiated for the first time by air.

End of winter storms were still playing havoc with weather in that area, and it was some time before aid came to the stranded airmen and they were flown out to New York. When it did come, it was only under the greatest difficulty that two Canadian bush pilots, "Duke" Schiller and Romeo Vachon, were able to reach Greenly Island and pick them up.

They were first flown to Murray Bay, on the north shore of the St. Lawrence River, where weather-bound American pilots awaited their coming, to fly them on to New York and celebrations they so greatly deserved.

The damaged *Bremen* was later dismantled and taken aboard ship, eventually to reach New York. Henry Ford decided such a sturdy craft deserved a place in history, an act which meant preservation for the craft and it was placed in the Ford Museum at Dearborn, Michigan, where it has remained to this day.

An historical aftermath of the daring adventure was the erection of a plain stone cairn on Greenly Island, at the expense of the Canadian Clarke Steamship Company, Limited. The shipping firm operate a passenger- and freight-carrying service in that area, and Greenly Island is a port of call for vacationers making cruises on their ships.

The dedication of the cairn was performed on July 25, 1928, the unveiling being performed jointly by Monseigneur Laventoux, Roman Catholic Bishop of the North Shore, Reverend Father Gallix and the Anglican representative, Canon F. G. Scott. Cruise passengers from the S.S. *North Shore* also attended, together with the ship's captain, L. A. Brie, and crew members. A large turnout of fishermen and their families from areas nearby were also on hand for the ceremony.

Commendation is due to Clarke Steamships for the prompt manner in which they arranged to have the cairn erected, and it is on record as the first such marker anywhere to be built and dedicated to record any North Atlantic flight. On the bronze plaque attached to the cairn is the following brief account of the flight:

On this island landed the *Bremen* on Friday, April 13, 1928, after the first nonstop flight of the Atlantic from east to west, having left Ireland at dawn on Thursday, April 12. Members of the crew were Baron Gunther von Huenefeld of Germany, Captain Hermann Koehl of Germany, Major James C. Fitzmaurice of Ireland. Erected by Clarke Steamship Co., Ltd., Montreal, Quebec, in recognition of a very gallant feat.

25. A Majestic Visitor from England

AIRSHIP FLIGHTS ACROSS the North Atlantic began in July, 1919, with the return crossing of the British R-34 from England to New York and back.

Such flying is not comparable with airplane flights, as the entire method is different. Airship travel was then considered a reasonably safe means of travelling by air, certainly more so than by airplane, but up to the time of the R-100's visit to Canada none of the monstrous craft had ever touched down in the Dominion or in Newfoundland.

The establishment of airship routes connecting the widely separated parts of the British Empire had been under consideration by the British government for several years, because in some quarters it was believed the use of airships might assist in welding the Commonwealth closer together.

As far back as June, 1927, the Canadian government had passed an Order-in-Council to acquire land in eastern Canada, for the establishment of an airfield which could also accommodate airships. A site was eventually chosen seven miles from the centre of the city of Montreal, at St. Hubert, where the huge airport is in use today.

Two British airship experts, Major G. H. Scott, original commander of the R-34, and Mr. A. R. Gibbs, were sent to Canada to look over the various sites, and the one at Montreal was considered to be the best. By the end of November, 1927, clearing the huge area of farm buildings, fences and bush was well advanced, and a permanent road to it from the city had been completed. Then came the massive job of erecting the airship mooring mast, and it was on the way by the spring of 1929.

The word "mast" is quite a misnomer, and very misleading. The immense bulk of British or other airships required something equally appropriate to moor them to. The masts were no mere flagpoles to which an aircraft could be tied. Actually, they were great steel towers, impressive in themselves. They contained every conceivable convenience for quickly mooring an airship to them, and for servicing the big ships once they were attached.

The Montreal mast was built as one of the Empire links, and further details about it are interesting. Once the steel tower structure had been assembled, the tower head had to be built on top. Most of the St. Hubert tower was fabricated in Montreal, but the airship handling machinery was manufactured in England, together with several others destined for use on masts erected in India, Egypt and one for Australia, which was never built.

The mooring equipment operated by electricity, as did a large elevator for use in transporting people and supplies between ground level and the tower head. Powerful pumps at the base enabled fuel to be forced up pipes to the top, where connection was made through fittings in the nose of the airship. That is the way the fuel and water tanks of the craft were replenished. A silicol-process hydrogen plant was nearby, capable of producing 40,000 cubic feet of gas an hour, and an adjacent gasometer held an additional 50,000 cubic feet.

All this vast preparation was not intended just for the visit of the R-100. It meant that Montreal could expect to become a vital airship link around the world.

Lieutenant-Commander A. B. Pressy was put in charge of Canada's only airship base and, together with four navy ratings, he was sent to England to undergo eighteen months of training duties at the Cardington Royal Airship Works. This was done to enable the five men to become familiar with the procedure in ground handling of the huge airships. They later returned to Canada to train others.

Specially trained radio and meteorological staffs were readied, and suitable buildings and equipment were provided. Altogether, the preparations for the first visit of an airship to Canada were carefully planned, most complete and very expensive.

His Majesty's Airship, the R-100, captained by Commander R. S. Booth, was selected to make the flight from England to Canada, and its arrival at Montreal touched off what was undoubtedly the greatest single air event ever to take place in the Dominion, considering the wide publicity it received and the consequent intense public interest from coast to coast.

The Federal and Quebec governments realized this ahead of time, to their credit, and knowing that huge crowds would be drawn to St. Hubert, the precautions they established to prevent traffic jams were almost fantastic. Military and police departments were briefed to properly direct and handle the crowds to come, and a new siding and platform were built by the Canadian National Railway on tracks adjoining the airfield. This was done to accommodate the passengers who would be coming and going by train from many points, as well as Montreal. Highways were put into first-class condition on all approaches for miles away, and connections with the new harbour bridge over the St. Lawrence were rushed to completion.

It was a good thing that such intensive precautions were taken because it was conservatively estimated that over one million people visited St. Hubert Airport during the ten days the R-100 was there. Over 5,000 had the opportunity of going through the ship as it was moored to the mast. After it was all over the airport record books showed 3,000 landings and takeoffs had been recorded by visiting aircraft.

The original date set for the airship's arrival was in the spring of 1930 but, due to various circumstances, the final plan called for the crossing in July.

The majestic craft left her Cardington base in England at 3.30 a.m. on July 29, 1930, on what was the start of her maiden voyage. Favourable weather prevailed until the Canadian coast was reached, where a storm of unusual violence was encountered over the St. Lawrence River near Three Rivers, Quebec. During the battle with the elements the fabric covering was badly torn on the underside of the huge portside stabilizer fin but the craft went on to Montreal at reduced speed, arriving during the night of July 31st.

Circling the city until dawn, she then crept slowly towards the mast where a perfect hook-up was established. She was attached to the tower at 5.00 a.m. on August 1st, which gave the time of her log from Cardington to Montreal as 78 hours and 52 minutes for the full journey. Slow of course compared with the speeds of airplanes, but at that date it constituted a record crossing for an airship.

Top officials were on hand to greet Commander Booth, his officers, and crew. The firm of Vickers Limited, of Montreal, was given the job of repairing the huge rent in the port fin. It was work which required the affixing of several tremendous fabric panels, each of which was twenty feet square. Their size affords some idea of the R-100 as a whole, as the fin actually was a tiny portion of the whole majestic ship. She was 700 feet in length.

The patches had to be prepared with thousands of eyelets along their edges for lacing them on, and they were in readiness by August 2nd. Together with almost 500 smaller patches, which had to be cemented in place, the repairing went forward without delay and was finished by the 8th.

On the next day the craft cast off from the mast, to get under way for a leisurely cruise over Canadian territory, which carried her along the St. Lawrence and over the Ottawa valley. Military, Air Force and government officials were aboard as guests, together with other public notables and members of the press.

Reaching Ottawa after darkness had fallen, her huge bulk showed clearly against the starlit summer sky. Practically every person in the nation's capital was outdoors to witness the event. A two-way radio communication system between the airship and radio station CNRD was maintained, the resultant hook-up enabling hundreds of thousands of Canadians to listen-in on the conversations between the ship and the ground. As she slowly circled at a low altitude above the Parliament Buildings, six powerful searchlights played upon her silver sides, making an impressive picture which no one who saw it will ever forget.

From Ottawa, the R-100 flew over parts of eastern Ontario during the night, but few people knew of her passing as she slipped by almost silently, high overhead. Dawn found her following the Canadian shoreline of Lake Ontario on an easterly course, and by 6.00 a.m. she was cruising over Niagara Falls. Turning back, the craft was headed for Toronto, and at greatly reduced speed she circled over the Queen City at 9.00 a.m., completely disrupting morning rush-hour traffic on the downtown streets which were soon black with people.

In leisurely fashion the trip was then completed back to Montreal, where she arrived at noon, and the intricate job of mooring to the mast was again handled with great efficiency. Work then got under way immediately to ready the airship for the return to England, and at 9.30 p.m., on August 13th, she was released from the tower and rising slowly to avoid all local obstructions she circled the field once and then headed into the east for home.

The full crew complement of the R-100 was forty-two men, the additional thirteen passengers aboard being made up of officials, and the press. By noon of August 14th, passengers and crew of the R-100 bade good-bye to Canada, as the airship stood out to sea and Belle Isle passed out of sight astern. Little did they realize it then that they had seen the start and the end of airship development in Canada.

The intense interest throughout Great Britain and Canada, which the visit of the ship aroused, made it then seem that the era of tremendous development by airships was on the threshold, but such was not to be.

Accidents to several of the world's largest airships belonging to Germany, Great Britain and the United States, which took place in the following five years, with the loss of hundreds of lives, sounded the death sentence for all such big craft. To date there has been no indication that they will ever return for use as commercial ventures, but there is belief in some quarters that the big airships may stage a comeback in the future.

The mooring tower at St. Hubert stood for many years as a melancholy reminder, unused and useless. Then as the airfield gradually developed into a tremendously busy and important airport, the structure became a menace to airplanes using the runways, and in 1933 the order was issued to have it demolished.

The huge sum of money which was involved in its construction, together with all the additional services, may seem to have been wasted when we look at things today but at the time it was built no one realized that the big airships were to pass completely out of the flying picture, as reliable, large and fast flying airplanes were developed, to oust them from the skies perhaps for ever.

26. The Long Way to London

IN 1931, AND FOR the first time on record, a Canadian-built and registered airplane had a go at flying the Atlantic. On this occasion, however, it was the South Atlantic, not the North Atlantic, that met with defeat, and that long risky over-water hop was but a small part of the full journey the aircraft made.

Eight months before the flight began a well-known Australian airman named Bert Hinkler, arrived in Toronto, Ontario, and placed an order with the De Havilland Aircraft Company of that city for a specially built Puss Moth monoplane.

As the work progressed Hinkler spent most of his time in the factory keeping an eye on things and making suggestions here and there the way he wanted things done. One thing in particular he specified was a huge fuel tank in the main body of the machine. It was so huge, the fuselage was actually constructed around it as the work progressed. Its large size, and consequential big fuel capacity, meant only one thing, the airman had plans in mind to fly long distances nonstop.

Speculation among the plant employees was rife, many believing Hinkler planned to fly from Toronto nonstop to some point in Europe, but the airman just smiled when asked and kept mum on the subject.

By October, 1931, the Puss Moth was completed and received Canadian registration lettering, CF-APK and, after a few test flights, Hinkler expressed great satisfaction with its performance in the air.

159

With everything working smoothly, he left Toronto on October 20th, flying directly to New York, although there were still some who believed he would next be heard from thousands of miles away. So modest were his actions, not even the newspapers were informed, and only a few friends and some of the De Havilland staff were on hand to see him off.

With full fuel tanks his machine could stay in the air for twenty-five hours without landing, as it cruised along at a speed of 110 miles per hour. A quick bit of figuring works that out to show he could cover approximately 2,750 miles in calm air, if he chose to do so, without a stop anywhere.

The Australian was not after speed records, neither was he planning to make a hurried nonstop flight attempt, so he took his time at the various places he stopped, acting like an ordinary tourist, taking in all the sights such localities had to offer.

When flying, he depended on keeping a correct course by visual sight with the ground. With a huge batch of maps, torn out of an ordinary school atlas, he set off on the second lap of his epic journey, leaving New York on October 26th, just as inconspicuously as he had stolen away from Toronto.

That he had supreme confidence in the machine and his own flying ability is proved by the fact that he set a direct course for the West Indian island of Jamaica, across open water, 1,472 miles away.

On the morning of the 27th, at eight o'clock he landed at Kingston, much to the great surprise of the residents who knew nothing of his coming. In doing so he established a record for the Island, because no wheel-equipped airplane had previously landed on Jamaican soil on a flight from America.

As he flew through the darkness of that October night, Hinkler's method of navigation was unique. As the flight was over water, he had to rely entirely on compass bearings for direction. Weather was fairly clear, and the moon was almost at the full, but occasionally he flew through cloud formations. On emerging into the moonlight from such experiences, he would circle his machine to get the moon behind him, so that its light would fall upon the instrument board and compass. After a quick check to learn if everything was running all right he would swing back to his course and continue on. The reason he was obliged to do this, was because he had not fitted his craft with electric dash-lights, having sacrificed their use so that he could eliminate the heavy weights of a generator and battery which would otherwise have been necessary.

After a week's stay in Jamaica, he was off again, angling southeast, 600 miles across the Caribbean Sea, to a landing on the South American continent, at Maracaibo, Venezuela. Still in no great hurry, the airman stayed several days, and then flew to the British-owned island of Trinidad, situated off the northeast coast of Venezuela, arriving November 10th.

In this leisurely fashion, he covered something like two thousand miles along the equatorial northern coast of South America, touching at numerous points, which included George-town, British Guiana; Cayenne, French Guiana; and Para, Brazil. He reached the city of Natal, Brazil, on November 20th, at about the most eastward point of the continent.

Then came preparations for the flight across the South Atlantic, *which no one had ever flown across alone before.* It was a formidable task for a small plane such as owned by Hinkler, but the afternoon of November 26th found him on his way, speeding over the 1,700 miles of ocean wastes between Natal, and French West Africa. Bad weather plagued him on this dangerous journey, which continued through the night and well on into the following day. When he finally arrived at Bathurst, Gambia, on the African coast, he had been 22 hours in the air under rugged flying conditions.

As his route now turned northward, the airman realized he would be running into winter conditions so all at once he was in a hurry. After only a brief stop at Bathurst, just enough to refuel his machine, he was off again and managed to make 200 miles up-coast to St. Louis, at the mouth of the Senegal River, before darkness overtook him on the 27th. His planned destination was London and, with climatic conditions becoming increasingly worse as he headed north, the airman did not tarry along the way whenever weather permitted him to get into the air and keep to a set course.

By the 29th he had flown along the very desolate and sparsely populated coast of West Africa to reach Casablanca, Morocco, with only one stop at Port Etienne on the way. On December 1st, he crossed the Strait of Gibraltar and reached Madrid in central Spain, going on the next day to Paris, France.

The bad weather he had expected proved to be lying in wait, and he was grounded for three days in the French capital. Then on the 5th he made a bid to reach London but dense clouds hemmed him in on all sides, so he was obliged to go down to a landing at Tours, to remain there until the 7th.

Then the great day came at last, when he flew on over the English Channel to a landing at Henworth Airport, on the outskirts of London. Thus the long and arduous flying journey over many thousands of miles of almost every conceivable type of terrain came to a conclusion, accomplished in an elapsed time of forty-eight days.

The staunch Puss Moth worked perfectly throughout the entire undertaking. Proof of whether it was a real adventure or not can best be judged by the fact that the British Aeronautical Society awarded to Bert Hinkler the Seagrave Memorial Trophy for 1931 ". . . for having accomplished the most daring flight of the year." The presentation was made in London in 1932.

Because Hinkler was such an experienced pilot the tragic circumstances which brought to an end the famous Australian's flying career have a part in this narrative.

By January of 1933, he had completed plans to fly his Puss Moth from England to Australia, in an effort to break the then existing record of 8 days, 20 hours and 44 minutes. He took off from near London on January 7th, with the avowed intention of flying nonstop to Brindisi, at the southern tip of Italy, on the Adriatic coast.

When he failed to reach his destination, and the hours stretched into days, it was realized that dire misfortune had engulfed him somewhere along the way. An air search was made, but no one knew for sure where to look for him, and it proved in vain. It was not until melting snows in the Italian mountains revealed what had happened, when his body and the burned-out wreckage of the Puss Moth were discovered near the top of one of the high peaks of the Apennine Range, not far from Pratomagno, in central Italy.

Thus on the winter slopes had been written *finis* to a daring Australian air man and his sturdy Canadian-built plane. They had battled it out together against the elements for sixteen months, and so they perished together, deep in a foreign country, both of them far from their native land.

27. To Canada over Greenland's Glaciers

DURING THE EARLY CONQUEST of the Atlantic Ocean by air, a few fortunate pilots earned everlasting fame and some a tidy fortune, but by the middle of the nineteen thirties the glory and pleasant financial rewards had dwindled to almost nothing.

There was mighty little left to gain when the British pilot John Grierson first tried, and failed, in 1933 and then was successful when he had another stab at it in 1934. On his second attempt he made the hazardous journey from London all the way to New York, his reward consisting of his own satisfaction in having accomplished it.

He was the first airman to fly alone from England to the United States, via the Iceland-Greenland-Canada route, and his efforts reflect great credit to him. His solo hop across the 450 miles over the Greenland icecap should have earned for him much more recognition and laurels than he ever received.

On his first attempt, and on the later successful one, he flew what were then, and are now, termed light aircraft, single engined machines built for pleasure-flying, not for the risks involved in Atlantic attempts.

In 1933 he made his first effort when he took off from Brough, on the east coast of England, heading north for Scapa Flow, at the tip of Scotland. He was flying a small De Havilland Moth seaplane, painted red and black, and named by Grierson the *Rouge et Noir*. He chose the name from the two colours of a roulette wheel which he considered coincided with the gamble he was taking on the flight.

After experiencing much difficulty in scraping together funds to launch his project, he started on August 4, 1933, and reached his Scottish destination safely. Then he flew across the wide ocean gap to the Faroe Islands and on to a landing at Reykjavik, Iceland. Both were long over-water hops for such a small machine, the longest being 500 miles and quite as risky as the open water of the North Atlantic itself.

Then bad luck hit him. During an attempt to take off for Greenland a big sea swell smacked the floats so hard it capsized his tiny ship, damaging it so badly it was beyond immediate repair. With a sad heart, Grierson arranged to have the seaplane shipped back to England, and returned with it aboard ship.

Having experienced the thrill of near success, he had an irrepressible determination to try again. Although badgered at every turn in financing and organizing the second attempt, he finally made it and was able to procure a sturdier aircraft than the original Moth. This time it was a De Havilland Fox Moth seaplane, single engined like the other, and Grierson gave it the name of the *Robert Bruce*, after the Scottish king of "Try, try again" fame.

By the middle of July, 1934, he was set once again for the great adventure, but this time he planned to go by a different route. From the tip of Ireland to Iceland is 750 miles across open Atlantic water, and Reykjavik is 810. As the mass flight of twenty-four Italian Savoia-Marchetti flying-boats had successfully negotiated that route in 1933, Grierson foresaw no difficulty for himself. Maybe he shut his mind to the fact each of the Italian machines had two powerful engines, and that the flying-boats were of seagoing type—and, more important still, that there was safety in numbers.

That he was flying alone did not daunt him a bit, and he pushed off on July 20, 1934, from the estuary of the River Thames at Rochester, Kent, the nearest seaplane base to London. His first lap took him nonstop to Londonderry, Ireland, the same port from which the Italians had flown from to Iceland the previous

year.   His plane was so fully loaded with fuel on the 23rd he had
a hard time getting up from the water but he finally made it,
leaving Ireland behind at Fanod Head, at 7 00 a.m.

Good weather was with him, and ten hours later the happy
airman landed close off shore from Reykjavik.   Taxiing to the
same wharf he had used in 1933, he tied up, and things looked
rosy for the future.   How wrong he was.   Apparently Iceland
held a hoodoo for him.   When he attempted to take off for Greenland several days later, he could not get off the calm water in the
fiord, so he went out around a point of land to open water, and
there his seaplane hit an anchored boat invisible from the cockpit.
A wing was smashed, and a float badly holed.

Grierson was then obliged to leave the Fox Moth at Reykjavik, and return to England by ship, to arrange for the purchase
of a new wing and to have repairs made to the float.   The latter
he took back with him for expert repairs at the Short Brothers'
factory at Rochester.   Delays stacked up one after the other, and
it was August 16th before he got back to Reykjavik, with a new
wing and the mended float.   Working like a Trojan, he had the
Robert Bruce flyable by the 19th.

Grierson made one short test flight on the day he finished the
job, and then on the 20th he finally set off for Greenland, no
doubt with a huge sigh of relief to see Iceland vanish astern.
Weather was kind to him, and he made the 480-mile over-water
trip across the Denmark Strait without difficulty.   Then trouble
loomed up in a frightening manner.

The east coast village of Angmagsalik had been his objective,
but on reaching the desolate Greenland coast, he had no idea
whether the settlement was north or south.   After fruitlessly
flying around, looking in vain for some sign of habitation, the
horrible truth burst like a bombshell—he was hopelessly lost!

Having luckily spotted a fiord which looked sufficiently free of
ice to leave room for landing, the airman sent out an S.O.S.
Finally he went down to a safe landing on the floe-cluttered fiord
to debate with himself just what to do, not knowing whether
anyone had picked up his call for help.   There was still three

hours' flying time left, as shown by the fuel gauge, so his predicament was not too bad if he only knew where to go, and he had emergency food rations to last ten days.

If his radio message had not been picked up by an alert operator at Angmagsalik, Grierson might well have perished, because there is no more desolate place on earth than the spot where he was down. The ease with which a pilot can become lost in that area is proved by the fact that he flew almost over the settlement on one circling flight and never spotted a thing. Sharp eyes below had seen him, however, and a search for him was soon under way as his S.O.S. had also been intercepted.

Pastor Rosing of the village Mission set off in a small power boat with six Eskimos in an effort to locate the airplane. All night they searched and well into the next day, going into every bay and inlet as they slowly progressed north in the direction they thought the plane to be. At last they came across Grierson and the *Robert Bruce*, in Agerderdussog Fiord, only twenty miles in an airline from the village. The hoodoo that so far had dogged the British airman was beginning to fade.

After having a rough map drawn for him by Pastor Rosing, to show the location of Angmagsalik Grierson was quickly on his way, reaching the settlement in quick time and hours ahead of the returning search party.

On August 23rd, and again on the 24th, Grierson made starts to fly over the icecap, but each time he was balked by dense clouds, and wisely turned back. It was a hazardous attempt for a small aircraft such as the Fox Moth with its single engine, and certainly no place for a seaplane to fly over under the best of conditions.

The 25th broke clear and sunny, and the airman was soon winging his way towards his goal on the west coast. When approaching the tremendously rough barrier of the icecap's edge and flying at 8,000 feet, the engine suddenly quit cold. Grierson suffered a lifetime of anguish in a few seconds as he began his glide down, knowing full well that there was not a drop of open water for him to land on, but only rugged rocks and the crevassed edge of the glaciers. Wondering desperately why the engine had stopped, he suddenly realized he had not switched on the tap from the main fuel tank after shutting of the auxiliary tank at the top of the climb. With a heartfelt prayer, he gave the tap a flip and immediately he heard the engine break into song, which to him sounded like the most beautiful music ever composed.

Little things like that can happen to the most cautious pilot, and Grierson was lucky to have been flying high which gave him time to think as he glided down, and to act. After that one heart-stopping episode, he went on to reach Godthaab, on the west coast of Greenland, without further strain and earned recognition of being the first pilot to ever fly across the Greenland icecap alone.

Forty-six years before, the explorer Nansen, together with a hardy group of fellow adventurers, had been the first to cross the Greenland icecap, doing so afoot on a treacherous journey which took forty-two days. Their crossing had been a tremendous ordeal, made about fifty miles to the south of the route followed by Grierson.

His machine was running perfectly, and on the 27th, after being gale-bound for one day, he flew from Greenland across the Davis Strait to his first landing on Canadian territory. The 650-mile hop took him to Lake Harbour, a Hudson's Bay Company post situated on the north shore of Hudson Strait.

After being suitably entertained by the company men and members of the R.C.M.P. stationed there, his next flight was to another Company post at Povungnetuk, 380 miles away on the east coast of Hudson Bay, where he arrived on the 28th.

Now the airman seemed in a hurry, and on the 29th, he flew first to the post at Fort George, a 480-mile trip, and then carried on another 110 miles to Eastmain, on the eastern coast of James Bay.

Luck was really favouring him at last. He arrived at Fort George only fifteen minutes after an offshore wind had dissipated a dense fog which had been hanging over the whole area for two days. If the country had still been fogbound when he arrived in the vicinity, he would almost certainly have become lost and, with practically no fuel left, he would have been in a bad predicament indeed. His emergency equipment at this time had been increased by order of the R.C.M.P. Besides rations for ten days, a rifle and fifty rounds of ammunition, he also had suitable fishing tackle.

The success of almost all of the early northern flights in Canada can well be credited in part to the aid given airmen at various Hudson's Bay Company posts throughout the country. Whenever an airman showed up, food, accommodation and fuel were offered without reservation, and flying visitors were always welcomed with open arms and every hospitality. The treatment Grierson received was no exception.

August 30th was a day to remember for the airman. After bidding good-bye to the kind people at Eastmain he flew a direct course to Ottawa, right across the forested wilderness of northern Ontario.

Weather had turned against him and he had a rough trip, but finally he set the floats of the *Robert Bruce* down to a landing on the Ottawa River near the R.C.A.F. Rockcliffe Air Station and there he became their guest.

Station personnel went to work on the somewhat battered looking Fox Moth and soon had it in good flying trim. As the flight to his destination of New York was over land, wheels were procured from the De Havilland factory at Toronto to replace the floats.

On September 10th Grierson was again in the air, heading for Albany, N.Y., and after refuelling there he flew on to New York the same day. Not long after his arrival at Curtiss Field several mechanics were looking into the open cockpit of the machine, when one remarked, "Say, guys, look at the instruments, there's enough of 'em there to fly the ocean." Grierson, standing nearby, overheard the quip and, turning to them, said, "You're right fellows, she has." There was silence for a few moments, then one of the men asked casually, "What ocean?" "The Atlantic," replied the airman. They looked at him with disbelief showing on all their faces, and as they walked away, one of them remarked with unveiled sarcasm, "Oh yeah, tell that to the Marines."

That is how John Grierson and the *Robert Bruce* arrived in New York unheralded and unsung, but he did not mind a bit. He had accomplished the job he had set his mind on doing for two years, overcoming some mighty big obstacles along the way on a flight which carried him 4,570 air miles from London to New York.

In due time he sailed back to England on the R.M.S. *Mauritania*, with the *Robert Bruce* below in the hold.

Eventually, he sold the sturdy Fox Moth to a gold-mining syndicate who procured it for use in New Guinea, but when he did so, Grierson freely admits, it brought a pang to his heart and he never saw his beloved craft again.

28. "Trail of the Caribou"

A CANADIAN NAMED Leonard G. Reid, born in Montreal in 1900, whose parents were Sir William and Lady Duff Reid, was destined to follow in the footsteps of his famous grandfather, although not exactly along the same lines.

Reid's grandparent acquired his fame as a Canadian railway and bridge builder, and among the large jobs he accomplished was the first bridge to span the St. Lawrence River between the City of Quebec and Levis on the south shore.

His grandson, Leonard, also bridged a wide gap of water, but of much greater span, because the job he undertook was to cross the Atlantic, but he did it by air. His partner on the project was pilot James R. Ayling, and between them they made a splendid nonstop flight from Canada to England. Ayling was born in India, his parents being Sir William and Lady Bock Ayling who at that time were living at Berhampur, south of Calcutta.

The circumstances which led Reid and Ayling to take part in the saga of Atlantic flying started in England when the famous English airman, Jimmy Mollison, and his equally well-known pilot wife, Amy, had flown across the North Atlantic from an actual takeoff point in Wales to a crash landing at night near Bridgeport, Connecticut.

Their twin-engined De Havilland Dragon Rapide biplane, the *Seafarer*, had been completely destroyed when they mistook the long line of lights on a Bridgeport highway for the city's airport runway. After their recovery from the injuries they received, the Mollisons procured a brand-new machine of the

171

type in which they had crashed, naming it *Seafarer II*, and in it they planned to fly back to England. Their final arrangements did not materialize, however, and the new machine went into storage at the Toronto factory of the De Havilland Company.

In 1934, Reid and Ayling purchased the *Seafarer II*, and renamed it the *Trail of the Caribou*, perhaps because of the long distances the Canadian caribou herds are known to travel, as they migrate thousands of miles in their search for new feeding grounds.

The two airmen first flew the Dragon Rapide from Toronto to Wasaga Beach, a summer resort on Canada's Georgian Bay. Plans for their forthcoming flight were carefully made, and it soon became public knowledge that they were out to make an attempt to beat the world's nonstop long-distance flying record.

Their hope was to fly without a stop to the ancient city of Baghdad, thousands of air miles away in far off Iraq. Even today it would be quite a fantastic flight in a similar type aircraft, for it means flying across eastern Canada, out over the North Atlantic to Europe, along the entire length of the Mediterranean Sea, over France, Italy, Greece and Turkey to finally reach Iraq and its central city of Baghdad. That is a long, long way.

On August 8, 1934, they were off on their great adventure, barely making it as the fully-laden airplane could hardly be induced to lift from the hard-packed sandy beach. An offshore wind crossing their line of takeoff made it a risky affair, and thousands of spectators stood by with bated breath as they watched the drama unfold. The suspense was terrific as the heavy-fuelled machine rushed towards the end of its runway, and it became touch and go whether the airmen were going to make it or end in a blazing crack-up.

At last the *Trail of the Caribou* lifted soggily into the air and cleared the treetops. Then a great shout went up from the crowd who let go their suppressed feelings with a tremendous cheer as the plane climbed into the eastern sky, and they saw the airmen were safely on their way.

All airplanes fly more economically at a reasonably high altitude where thinner air offers less resistance and where suitable tail winds may often be found to help them along. So the airmen climbed to a considerable height before levelling off on a straight flight. It was their undoing. They encountered freezing temperatures and the cold froze the engine throttle controls at a wide open setting.

It was serious from a fuel consumption point of view, and a most unfortunate hitch in the airmen's plans. The recognized thing to do, once a desired altitude has been reached, is to throttle back the engine sufficiently to hold the airplane at a set cruising speed, with the consequent conservation of precious fuel.

In their predicament the airmen, finding the throttle jammed, were unwilling to force it, believing that in doing so it might become bent and cause the engines to slow down if the fuel supply became limited and it could not be further controlled. If that happened it meant a fast trip down into the sea, so to avoid taking chances they left the throttle as it was, wide open. Every hour of their flight they used up seventeen gallons of fuel instead of the ten gallons an hour they had planned for cruising consumption. This forced the airmen to completely change their original plans and a destination in England was selected, the attempt on a very long distance nonstop being abandoned.

From the moment they left Wasaga Beach until they touched down in England on August 9th, at Heston Airport in Middlesex, they had been in the air for thirty hours and fifty-five minutes.

Check of the fuel tanks after they had landed, revealed there was still over 200 gallons of gas left, but it would not have been nearly enough to have carried them on to Baghdad. Even so, they had done very well. Their flight established a record for being the first made from west to east across the Atlantic, from a point on the Canadian mainland to a landing in England.

Not until after the outbreak of World War Two did similar flights become regular happenings, when pilots began ferrying fighter and bomber aircraft from Canada across the ocean to the various battlefronts.

It is nice to know that Canadians thought enough of the Reid and Ayling flight to have a suitable monument built to record it

close to the spot at Wasaga Beach from where it began.   The
brief wording on the bronze plaque attached to the stone cairn
contains tangible tribute to a brilliant flying achievement.
It reads:

HISTORIC SITES AND MONUMENTS
BOARD OF CANADA

From Wasaga Beach on the morning of 8th August,
1934, James R. Ayling and Leonard G. Reid took
off in their plane, *The Trail of the Caribou*, headed
for Baghdad.   Due to adverse weather conditions,
and exhaustion of fuel supplies, they were forced to
land at Heston Airfield, London, England, on the
afternoon of 9th August, having flown 3700 miles in
30 hours, 55 minutes.

Visitors to Wasaga Beach, who stroll over to look at the cairn,
become quite impressed when they read the brief legend.   They
receive quite a thrill as they stand there, and realize that in 1934,
two British airmen sped away from that very spot, and the next
time their feet touched down on solid ground they then stood on
the soil of England.

29. West with the Night

THE PILOT OF THE trim Percival Vega Gull monoplane, flying at a low height in the heart of Africa, circled continually over the sun-baked veldt, scanning the landscape below much like a strong-winged vulture.

The search was on, looking for signs of elephants, lions or water buffalo, so that a correct report of their number and location could be learned. The knowledge gained was quickly flown back to a base camp, where a hunting party awaited the news. The pilot would then fly several of them to the vicinity where the big game had been spotted from the air, and trophies were usually successfully obtained with a minimum loss of time and effort by the not-too-athletically-inclined hunters.

At first thought such an experience does not seem to have the slightest connection with flying in Canada but wait, for of such remote circumstances history is sometimes made.

It really began much farther back than that. The parents of a little girl had moved from England to reside in Kenya Colony and the child, growing to womanhood, had married to become Mrs. Beryl Markham. In 1930 she learned to fly in England, and in the six years which followed she earned both her private and commercial pilot's licences.

It was during that period that some of her flying exploits were carried out in east-central Africa over the thickly infested big game country of the Uganda Protectorate and Tanganyika Territory. She was the pilot in the Percival Vega Gull on the game-spotting flights.

An adventurous young woman, she cast about for ways of utilizing her flying skill in other directions and made numerous flights between Africa and England with passenger payloads. So in six years, she had logged over 2,000 hours in the air and had gained a vast amount of flying experience to boot. She had had her eye on flying the Atlantic for some time, and when she broached the idea to the owner of the Vega Gull, Lord Carbery, that she be permitted to make the attempt he was at first against it. Knowing her ability as an airwoman, he finally gave in when she was in England with the machine at the end of a flight from Kenya in 1936.

It did not take long to make plans, and it was decided that the start should be made from the Royal Air Force airfield at Abingdon, in Berkshire.

The machine was christened the *Messenger*, and a number of additional fuel tanks were fitted into the cabin and connected to the main supply line. They took up all available space, as every ounce of fuel which could be carried would be needed to ensure a successful crossing.

Unlike many of the early Atlantic planes, the *Messenger* possessed no radio. Everything was ready by September 4, 1936, and at 6.50 p.m., in the gathering gloom of night, courageous Beryl climbed up into the cockpit and soon was flying west over the darkening countryside with the mighty Atlantic beckoning her onward for whatever fate held in store. Then the solid blackness of the night enfolded her, the tiny plane becoming a minute nothing in the vast space of the sky above the ocean waste.

Hour after hour her eyes scarcely left the flying instruments, and it required a stout nerve and expert flying ability to carry on. The weather was not good. Rain and storm beset her most of the night. She should perhaps have turned back to await better conditions, but that was not in her make-up and she did not falter.

Flying west with the night, she found daylight long in coming on the 5th, because the *Messenger* was doing its tiny best to fly away from the sun. However, full dawn came at last, and with it the sunshine, but Beryl was still a long long way from land.

In mid-afternoon she was at last thrilled beyond measure to see the dark outline of land on the distant horizon, and soon it resolved itself as the coast of Newfoundland.

It had been the young woman's hope and desire to fly non-stop to New York, but a check of the fuel gauge showed there was not sufficient to take her that far. Strong headwinds had been encountered most of the way across, and they had severely retarded the Vega Gull's speed. Too, the airwoman was becoming increasingly weary with the strain and the long battle against the elements, so she decided to make a landing at the first opportunity. At least she had joined the illustrious group of conquerors of the Atlantic.

Carrying on until the remaining fuel was almost gone, she had by that time reached Nova Scotia, and there she searched about for a suitable landing-place. It was now late in the afternoon, and she had already flown 2,700 miles. Cruising around, her choice settled on a smooth-looking area just inshore from Bauliene Cove on Cape Breton Island, which is the northern portion of Nova Scotia.

The tired young woman set her craft down to a perfect landing on a wide area of marsh grass, but the instant the wheels took the aircraft's weight they sank deep into the soft ground. What Beryl had thought to be a smooth hard grassy surface, turned out to be a treacherous slimy bog.

Almost the instant the *Messenger* touched down it was yanked to an abrupt stop. Up went the tail, and the nose buried itself deep in the muck. So came the climax to a man-sized feat by a daring young woman.

News of her arrival soon reached the ears of members of the Cape Breton Flying Club who quickly rallied to her aid by extricating the Gull from its undignified position. It was a difficult task they set out to do, hauling the craft out of the bog to the firmer ground along the shoreline, but a couple of days' work saw the job completed by laying planks on top of the mud and slowly manhandling the craft out. It had suffered no damage structurally although the engine was completely gummed up with

Cape Breton mud. The airplane was then placed aboard a barge which was towed to nearby Sydney, and an ocean-going ship carried the stout little plane back to England.

Eventually it went back to Africa, and continued in use for many years on its old job of game-spotting, and passenger-carrying, but not with Beryl as its pilot. As for her, she stands alone in her accomplishment, for no woman before her flight or since, has flown the North Atlantic alone from east to west.

As government restrictions now completely forbid solo non-stop flights directly across in single-engined aircraft, it is reasonable to believe that Beryl Markham's achievement will remain unbeaten for all time, as a particularly outstanding flying event and a shining example of courageous womanhood.

Part six / THE MAINSTAYS

30. The PBYs in
Peace and War

YEARS BEFORE THE outbreak of World War Two, a large twin-engined flying-boat had been designed and built in numbers by the United States firm of Consolidated Aircraft Corporation. Some were designed with wheels attached to the hull, making them amphibious aircraft. The letters PBY denoted the company's official reference, and the machines themselves were called Catalinas.

Their reliability, coupled with their very long nonstop flying range, quickly made them a welcome addition for use by many commercial air companies, and the U.S. Government and several foreign countries were making use of them long before the war clouds loomed. When hostilities began many PBYs were adapted to military use as they lent themselves at once for such work as long range, submarine-spotting flights and ship convoy duties from the air.

Some of these fine aircraft had been seen in Canada during the 1930's, and one PBY in particular made quite a name for itself and its crew. It was a PBY, purchased by the Russian government in New York, but the crew hired to fly it was formed of one Australian and four Canadian airmen. From New York it was flown to a base established at Coppermine in the Northwest Territories, right on the coast of the Arctic Ocean.

It then went into use to conduct a widespread search over vast, uninhabited northern areas, in an endeavour to find and rescue six men aboard a lost Russian aircraft. The big six-engined craft had been forced down somewhere in the Arctic regions, while attempting a nonstop flight from Moscow to Mexico City.   It was like looking for a pinprick in a circus tent. The huge monoplane had followed a route over the North Pole and then vanished without a trace.

Sir Hubert Wilkins, the famous Australian explorer, was in command of the PBY, his able pilot, co-pilot, engineer and radio operator being respectively Herbert Hollick-Kenyon, Silas Cheesman, Gerald Brown and Raymond Booth—all Canadian airmen.

Some 34,000 square miles of the Arctic wastes were covered by air as the search went on in areas where it was believed the missing airplane might be found, some flights going as far as the North Pole itself.   The long and risky flights, so diligently carried out, revealed no trace of the lost Russians and the Soviet government finally called the search off, realizing that their airmen had vanished for ever.

Throughout the years of World War Two Canada built many PBYs, doing so in two widely separated factories, one the Boeing plant at Vancouver, B.C., the other being Canadian Vickers at Montreal.   All Canadian-built PBYs were named Cansos.

As the large and powerful flying-boats were completed they were shipped or flown to all parts of the world to be assigned to duties of varying types, of which submarine-spotting was not the least.

After the British battleship H.M.S. *Hood* had been sunk in the North Atlantic by gunfire from the German battleship, *Bismarck*, it was the crew of a Canadian-built Canso which first spotted the damaged German ship after the battle.   Flying in wide circles, but at a safe distance away from the German guns, the crew of the flying-boat radioed their victim's position to the ships of the British Atlantic squadron.   Soon they were swarming to the kill and the *Bismarck* was sent to the bottom with almost all of her crew in the same way she had despatched the *Hood*.

The PBYs were large airplanes, with a length of sixty-three feet and a wing span of one hundred and four feet.   To give a better example of the wings from tip to tip, imagine seven automobiles lined up bumper to bumper. They form the equivalent wing length, and there you have it. Each of their two Pratt and Whitney radial engines developed twelve hundred horse power. The PBY was not designed for high speed, but for very long-distance nonstop cruising.

Fully loaded it lazied along at about 100 miles an hour, but it could carry on for thousands of miles at that steady clip. About 16,000 feet was the top height to which a PBY could climb fully loaded, which meant a complete weight of seventeen tons. Just to demonstrate what a long way a PBY could fly nonstop, imagine one taking off from Halifax, N.S., on the east coast of Canada, and flying all the way to Vancouver, B.C., on the Pacific coast, without a stop. That gives a good example of their value in peace and in war.

When the war was over large numbers of the versatile flying-boats became available for purchase by private and commercial flying organizations, and they were put to extremely good use on many missions and are still going strong as these pages are written.

The Hudson's Bay Company purchased one for use in transporting goods and company personnel to and from their isolated posts throughout the Canadian northland. They aptly named their Canso *Polar Bear*, and it served the company truly and well until it was retired through old age several years ago.

Another Canadian firm, The Photographic Survey Corporation Limited of Toronto, have also utilized Cansos on photographic and mineral surveys in many parts of Canada. The flying laboratories, as they are named, with many intricate and sensitive instruments aboard, fly back and forth over set routes, searching for valuable mineral deposits from the air.

One of the most astounding items of the electronic instruments they use is termed an electromagnetometer. Six feet or so in length, it has the appearance of an aerial bomb. Attached to a wire cable, it is trailed about 500 feet beneath the aircraft in flight.

The electromagnetic waves it emits strike down to the ground and penetrate to a depth of 300 feet before instantly returning to be picked up by sensitive receiving apparatus inside the aircraft.

In this manner, absolutely accurate record can be gathered telling of what may lie below the earth's surface, whether it be copper, tin, lead, nickel, iron, asbestos, uranium or many other minerals. That is the way prospecting is being done in the modern manner and valuable discoveries have already been recorded, with more coming in every day.

Some PBYs have been converted into passenger-carrying flying-boats for use in commercial operations, and many of the sturdy craft, mostly amphibians, are still majestically riding the skyways on such missions. It will be a bad day for many flying companies when their PBY's wear out for they are not being made any more, and the supply of surplus war Cansos has long played out.

For well over thirty years the Catalinas and the Cansos have been slugging it out in all parts of the world, and that is an extremely long period for any one type of airplane to have continued to be in solid demand. As flying develops in the future, faster passenger and air freight carriers will be the rule, but there will always be a place for craft of slower capabilities as their operating costs are far down the scale in comparison with their speedier sisters.

31. The "Gooney Birds"

THE DC-3 TWIN-ENGINED airplane is not of Canadian design or origin but for over two decades it has played a major role in Canadian flying affairs. As it is undoubtedly one of the most popular wheel type of airplanes ever to exist, it would be a bad breach of etiquette if some of the facts about it were not included here.

In peace and war they have penetrated to and landed in areas all over the world, where even a slow single-engined airplane would have great difficulty in getting in, and far more so in flying out. It has been the "gooney" exploits which have been accomplished by pilots flying DC-3's, which earned for the craft the nickname, "Gooney Bird," and the title fits it like a cookie fits a small child's hand.

A product of the Douglas Aircraft Company of San Diego, the first DC-3 rolled off the assembly line in 1936 and many thousands followed in its wake. It has a top speed which on occasion can top 200 miles an hour, but usually they are cruised at 185. When the demand grew for a twin-engined airplane of sturdy construction, but with phenomenal loading ability, the Douglas DC-3 was the result. It undoubtedly surpassed company expectations beyond anything they had vaguely hoped for, because it has since become a household word connected with aviation in almost every country in the world.

It is so universally used and known everywhere, that it has become a sort of standard amongst the airplane mainstays which are in use today, and it will undoubtedly remain so for many years to come.

Its use in Canada has been multifarious. Large and small airline organizations throughout Canada have utilized DC-3's on passenger routes or in connection with charter work, and an immense amount of air freighting has been done with them.

During World War Two and the Korean War, DC-3's were commissioned into service by the allied nations, and hundreds of thousand wartime missions were flown by them in all parts of the world. They carried men and supplies, and were converted into ambulance planes, many times in the midst of battle zones using runways which were so limited in landing and takeoff facilities as to be useless for less versatile craft. Canada used them to the full during the war, and since then the "Gooney Birds" have been flown to every part of the country and far beyond the Arctic rim.

Few regular air passengers have not flown at some time or other in a DC-3. It would be impossible to travel often by air and not come into contact with them as so many are still in service.

If the craft had not been so well adapted for its many types of use it would have become obsolete long ago with the keen competition now existing among airline companies throughout the world. There are thousands still in use and hundreds of them are in Canada, being operated by the government or civil organizations. A recent estimate by the Douglas Company revealed that there are more than 4,500 of them still going strong throughout the world.

For twin-engined aircraft, they can carry an extraordinarily heavy load if the demand arises. It is on record that during the war one lifted a load exceeding 34,000 lbs., and on another occasion, when evacuating people from a jungle village just ahead of the advancing Japs, seventy-four persons were jammed inside its bulging sides after all the seats had been discarded. They all stood, packed like matches in a box, but they were saved and that was all that mattered.

There is the story going the rounds about a Canadian bush pilot which is worth the telling. He had landed his DC-3 at the end of a routine trip out of the north and after taxiing to where the craft was to be serviced he switched off the engines. Instead of getting up to leave, his co-pilot caught him looking wistfully out of the window at another DC-3 parked alongside. Wondering if maybe he was feeling sick, the co-pilot asked him and received a vague, "No-o-o." "Well what the heck is wrong? Haven't you ever seen a DC-3 before?" was the next question. Then the pilot came alive, "Yep, I sure have," he said, "and it brings back memories. Y'know, when I was just a kid the first airplane I ever saw back home at Winnipeg was a DC-3." He paused, and added, "Now all these years later, here I am flying one."

32. The Strong-Built Harvards

DURING THE SIX YEARS of World War Two, between 1939 and 1945, thousands of different types of airplanes were manufactured in Canada. Huge factories were built to accommodate the work, and all over the country small firms contributed to the job by supplying all kinds of parts which went into the construction of the finished airplanes.

A great many different types of war planes were included in the work involved, each designed for some special purpose such as training, supply and troop carrying, observation, fighters, bombers, etc. It is not possible to include all of them in this book, so some of the most important types must suffice as a means of drawing attention to the wonderful job Canadian men and women contributed towards the defence of the Commonwealth during those bitter years of war.

The trim two-seater Moths have already been dealt with in Part IV and, as described, most of the Royal Canadian Air Force trainees of World War Two were first introduced to the thrills of flying in the cockpit of a Moth.

When a student pilot had become thoroughly used to flying a Moth it was necessary for him to undergo additional and more advanced training, in order to fit him for receiving his "Wings" and the final graduation to fly fighter or bomber aircraft.

Once a pupil had been certified competent by an instructor on an intermediate trainer type of airplane, he was at last ready to sit in the pilot's seat of the most advanced airplanes the Air Force had to offer.

From initial flight instructions in Moths, eager young men

under military training went on to flying Harvards, a much faster craft, which turned out fully qualified pilots. When the war started Canada had no Harvards of her own in service and was obliged to import many from the United States to fill the pressing need. The demand for the Harvard intermediate trainers became so great it was not long before the Canadian government subsidized various companies in Canada to build them, and soon they were turning them out in a steady stream for distribution to flying centres.

When the United States entered the war the picture changed, and a large number of Canadian-built Harvards were diverted to their needs for training men for the United States Army Air Force. At the Elementary Flying Training Schools which were established in Canada keen young men by the thousands arrived by ship loads from Australia, New Zealand and England to undergo flight and other instruction. Many trainees also came from countries already attacked or overrun by the German armies—Norway, Poland, Belgium, France—all being well represented, as well as others. All those fellows who were to become pilots eventually graduated from flying Harvards.

A two-seater airplane, and ideal for use as an intermediate trainer, it looked every inch a warplane and was perfect for instructing young pilots for the final phase of fighting in the air. Although the war has now been over many years, Harvards are still in use as military trainers in Canada and in many other countries as well.

Powered with a single air-cooled radial engine, with an output of 550 horsepower, top speed in the air is 220 miles an hour. It has a nonstop flying range of 870 miles and, fully loaded, can climb to an altitude of 23,000 feet. Unlike that of the Moth, the Harvard landing-gear is retractable, imparting to trainees at the controls the true feeling that he has graduated to fly a really modern machine. It is probable that Harvard trainers will survive for a long time for the work they are so well fitted to do. They have so fully proved their worth, and fit in so well with training requirements, there seems little need to switch to other types as long as the strong-built Harvards remain procurable.

33. The Mighty Lancasters

THE GREATEST AERIAL bomb-carriers possessed by the Royal Air Force before and during World War Two were the Avro-built four-engined Lancaster bombers. When fully loaded each machine could carry nine tons of bombs as well as the extra weight of crew, fuel and armament. The total weight of the mighty craft was then thirty-four tons.

Four powerful Rolls-Royce Merlin engines, totalling 6,440 horsepower, keep the monster in the air. With such a vast weight to lift, it would be forgivable to think that the propellers, even with so much power driving them, would not be able to pull the craft through the air at any great speed, but such a guess would be wrong. The Lancs could easily hit a top speed of over 250 miles an hour and, to add to that, their flying range on nonstop bombing raids or sweeps out over the Atlantic could carry them 2,600 miles.

Additional improvements as the war progressed gave them still more ability as more powerful engines were fitted and their air speed rose to over 300 miles per hour accordingly. Lancasters were one of the types of aircraft Canadian workers built during the war years, and at the huge Victory Aircraft Limited plant at Malton, near Toronto, hundreds of them were completed and commissioned for use.

Thrilling and heroic stories by the hundreds can be told by their aircrews and the manner in which the Lancasters could take severe punishment from enemy gunfire. Proof of their sturdy durability was of daily occurrence when on active service, for many came back from dangerous missions battered and torn by the tremendous barrages of ack-ack fire through which they had flown. To look at some of them after they had returned from combat with enemy fighter aircraft was to wonder how they had remained aloft at all. Bullet riddled, or torn almost apart by shell fragments from exploding flack, some would have gaping holes in their sides while others would have large portions of wings or tail sections missing. Often enough, a returned Lancaster looked more like a shattered old disused wreck rather than what had been a fine looking airplane a few hours before.

Although peace is now with us the Lancasters still ply the airways on numerous military missions but not in such great numbers as before. As each one of these big machines is retired from service simply from old age, there are no new ones of its type to take its place. Actually, they are now considered to be an obsolete type and as none are now being manufactured, it means that sooner or later they will be seen in the sky no more.

Some of the work carried out by these aircraft since the war has contributed valuable information of a scientific nature. Other flights of equal importance have been made in connection with search and rescue operations in many parts of the world and particularly in Canada and off our Atlantic and Pacific shores.

A British Royal Air Force Lancaster, with all warlike equipment removed and filled with scientific instruments instead, is just one instance. It took off from Prestwick, Scotland, on May 10, 1945, and arrived at Ottawa without undue publicity. Named the *Aries*, its crew's primary job was to fly over the Magnetic Pole area and accurately chart the exact position. This was done between May 19 and 26, 1945, and their research discovered the Magnetic Pole to be far removed from where it was previously thought to be. It was thought to be somewhere on Boothia Peninsula, far up in northern Canada, but the instruments aboard the *Aries* pinpointed the spot on Prince of Wales Island, which is about a thousand miles south of the North Pole itself.   After returning to the R.C.A.F. Station at Ottawa, to divulge the findings, the *Aries* was later flown nonstop, back to its home base in Scotland, the flight taking it directly over the Arctic regions and the North Pole itself.

In the past decade or so, Lancasters have taken part in so many search and rescue missions in various parts of Canada their name has become a household word and to many Canadians their appearance in the air is well known.   They are distinguishable from most other large airplanes with four engines by reason of the two vertical rudders, which are attached to the tail section on either side.

34. North Stars In the Sky

ALMOST EVERYONE with the least smattering of knowledge of the heavens knows that there is but one North Star in the sky— the Pole Star, to name it correctly. When the name is applied to aircraft, it is another story. There are hundreds of North Stars in the sky.

The huge Canadair Limited plant at Montreal is where the North Star aircraft are manufactured, and for years the company built the large four-engined machines. It has become a famous ship and has been purchased for use by private and government sources not only in Canada but in many other parts of the world.

The craft is designed for the air transport of passengers, and comfortable reclining seats within its big interior accommodate from forty to fifty persons at a time, depending on the seating arrangements which different airlines specify.

For a considerable number of years the Canadian government-owned Trans-Canada Air Lines used North Stars on their routes in Canada, as well as over the long distance flights serving Great Britain, the United States and Bermuda. Hundreds of thousands of satisfied passengers have enjoyed flying in the safe and well patronized air liners.

When loaded with a full complement of crew, passengers, baggage and fuel, the total weight of the entire machine is in the vicinity of forty-three tons, but in spite of that great weight the powerful engines, totalling approximately 10,000 horsepower, are capable of flying the craft at a speed of well over three hundred miles an hour. It has a long nonstop flying range, too. A North Star can travel a distance of almost 4,000 miles before it must land for fuel, if such a distance is required on scheduled or unscheduled flights.

Another large and well established Canadian flying company, Canadian Pacific Air Lines, has also favoured the use of North Stars for many years. During the Korean War Canadian Pacific Air Lines contracted with the United States government to fly military personnel and equipment from America to Japan. The route taken was by way of the Pacific, north to Alaska, then via the Aleutian chain of islands south to Tokio. Many thousands of American servicemen and servicewomen, were flown to Japan in North Stars. Millions of pounds of priority supplies and equipment were flown the same way. On their return flights to Canada and American points, wounded men, personnel on leave and officials connected with Korean operations were passengers. It was a splendid feather in Canada's "aviation cap" to have her pilots and aircraft entrusted with such vital work, and it was accomplished with a remarkably fine accident-free record and without fanfare.

Apart from such aid extended to war services, Canadian Pacific Air Lines also made general use of North Stars in connection with their commercial routes in Canada, and from Canada to Europe, South America, Mexico, Honolulu and Japan. In fact, wherever their aircraft operate, where it is necessary to utilize large aircraft, there you will find North Stars on the run.

The Royal Canadian Air Force also has good reason to be proud of the Canadair product. They have many North Stars in service carrying out daily duties, flying personnel to points all over Canada and to far distant lands. During the Korean War, the R.C.A.F. conducted similar airlift operations to those carried out by Canadian Pacific Air Lines between Canada and American points and Japan.

The squadron which did the work was designated as number 426 and was known as the "Thunderbirds." Thunder they surely did, flying across the world millions of miles and carrying tens of thousands of passengers and millions of pounds of freight, until the cessation of hostilities brought their North Star airlift to an end.

On January 14-15, 1949, a flight conducted by the crew of a Royal Canadian Air Force North Star, drawn from their Experimental and Proving Establishment, contributed a worthy record to Canadian flying history. After leaving Vancouver, B.C., the craft was flown nonstop to Halifax, N.S., in eight hours and thirty-two minutes. It was an accomplishment which had long been overdue, and it established the first record of an airplane having been flown completely across Canada nonstop from Vancouver to Halifax.

Since the Canadair company began turning out North Stars, not all of them by any means have gone into service in Canada. Civil and military organizations throughout the world have purchased them in numbers because of their reliability and sturdy construction.

In spite of all the advanced designs and many types to choose from, Great Britain turned to Canada for the purchase of a number of North Stars. It occurred when the world renowned British Overseas Airways Corporation selected a number of Canadair-built air liners for use on their many world air routes. Unfortunately for Canada, once that firm took delivery of their North Stars they were renamed Argonauts and they lost their true identity as a consequence, except for people in the know.

A signal honour won by the Canadair product was the choice by officials of B.O.A.C. of an Argonaut from their fleet of twenty-two such craft when they were requested by Buckingham Palace to supply a suitable airplane for Royal use in 1952. It was required to fly Princess Elizabeth and Prince Philip in connection with their lengthy tour planned as far as Australia, via Africa and way points.

The craft was already named the *Atlanta*, and it was duly preened and polished for the responsible job it was set aside for. Unfortunately the flying journey was interrupted in Africa, when the sad news of the death of H.M. King George VI reached the

Royal couple, and they were flown back to England at once in the *Atlanta*, when its duties of flying them to the Antipodes had scarce begun.

The throaty roar from the four exhausts of the powerful engines of a North Star—or Argonaut—are as well known by the public today as any of the big airliners which ply the air routes in many parts of the world. So many of these craft are now in regular use everywhere they have become well recognized by most airminded people. In Canada, never a day goes by but they are seen winging sturdily along high in the sky, and mighty few are the young people, or older ones, who on glancing up cannot say if they wish, "There goes a North Star."

35. Trucking along Our Aerial Highways

THE PIONEER WORK of the Fokker and Fairchild airplanes, described in Part IV, stamped them as the early workhorses of the air when commercial air trucking got its start in Canada in the 1930's.

Good as they were they eventually wore out and their place was filled by other types, which modern progress in design and more powerful engines made more suitable for handling larger payloads, while being able to fly much farther on nonstop missions.

One of the later additions for use in commercial and military transport was the Noorduyn Norseman, hundreds of which proved their worth in all parts of Canada. Many of them were built in Canada under licence from the parent American company, the work being done in the plant of Canadian Car and Foundry Co., Ltd., at Fort William, Ontario, which has since ceased such production.

The De Havilland Aircraft Company of Toronto entered the field of aerial trucking by designing and constructing the aptly named Beaver, a remarkably versatile aircraft.

Primarily, it was planned for use as a bush-flying machine, but was so adaptable in respect to other flying jobs that it became a universal airplane and has spread out for use in all parts of the world. It can haul an air cargo in the same way that trucks handle freight along regular highways, but because it is airborne it is infinitely better in many respects to its earthbound sisters.

It is also a passenger-carrier when desired, the seats being fitted in such a manner they can all be removed in twenty minutes, or replaced in the same time. As the craft is adaptable for use with wheels, floats or skis, it is ideal for meeting all climatic and geographical conditions.

Many such craft have been converted into air ambulances, and their consequent mercy flights in many countries have been legion in number and many have made the newspaper headlines.

With suitable equipment fitted, it becomes an aerial crop duster as a prevention against mildew or rust, and it is equally at home in the air, spraying poisonous chemicals over forested areas which are being attacked by blight or insect pests. Vast areas can be treated in double-quick time, and all such work has proved invaluable.

One of its latest uses is to aid forest-fire fighting, with large tanks fitted above either pontoon. They are filled automatically as the Beaver taxies across the surface of a lake or river. Then the machine is flown to the danger area and the water is dumped on the flames. It has proved to be an excellent method of extinguishing blazes before they get beyond human control.

During the Korean War the United States government purchased over six hundred Beavers from the De Havilland Company. They were used as reconnaissance and ambulance planes in Korea because of their fantastic ability to take off and land in incredibly confined areas.

One of the Beaver's outstanding abilities is to fly at an extremely slow air speed. It can be cut down to fly safely at less than 55 miles per hour at the will of the pilot, although it has a top speed of 115 miles an hour.

The choice of the Canadian-built Beavers by the United States government over all the types their own country had designed and built was a tremendous compliment to the Canadian air industry. When once a Beaver is commissioned for use on duty with the American armed forces it loses its Canadian identity and becomes simply an "L-20." Many are still in active use by the United States forces, in connection with military operations although the Korean War is long over.

Not only in Canada but in dozens of other countries to which Beavers have been sold their work goes on continually, and the Royal Canadian Air Force and the Royal Canadian Mounted Police make good use of them in connection with their varied operations throughout the Dominion.

The De Havilland Company, realizing the worth of the Beaver, set to and designed a big sister, planned along similar lines and choosing for it the name of another of Canada's wild animals, the Otter.

Larger in freight- and passenger-carrying capacity than the Beaver, the Otter is able to handle a total of fourteen people to the Beaver's seven, and it has a correspondingly more powerful engine. Also suitable for use on wheels, floats or skis, it can lift almost a ton weight of payload and, flying at 125 miles an hour, can reach out to distant points up to 800 miles away nonstop.

Today, as this book is written, Norsemen, Beavers and Otters, have taken over many of the major tasks which flying demands they fill, particularly as such work applies to out-of-the-way and off-the-beaten-track destinations where landing and takeoff facilities are extremely limited.

With hundreds of these machines now in daily use they have become a familiar sight in Canada, as they and their pilots so worthily contribute towards the progress of the country by trucking along our aerial highways.

36. Man-Made Dragonflies

ALTHOUGH HELICOPTER AIRCRAFT have only been fully perfected for use since the end of World War Two, they quickly filled a gap in air operations which was waiting for them because of many abilities which no other types of airplanes possessed.

By the men who fly them helicopters are always referred to as rotary wing aircraft because that is exactly what they are. In accounts in newspapers, and many other publications relating to them, helicopters are often described by such comical terms as "whirlybirds" or "flying egg-beaters" but such descriptions are not very kind, considering the splendid work they can accomplish.

A much better definition, if nickname must be used, would be to name them "man-made dragonflies." It is much closer to their operational methods and quite characteristic of what they can do. At a distance in flight they look for all the world like a huge dragonfly. Some, with their bulbous head and long thin body and their whirring almost invisible rotor blades, are huge replicas of a busy dragonfly on the wing.

They can take off from and land on "a dime," as the saying goes. Added to that they are able to come to a dead stop in the air and, at the pilot's will, can rise or lower slowly, while hovering over a selected position. If the pilot wishes, he can pivot the craft completely around on its own axis while hovering. It can be understood then that describing a helicopter as a man-made dragonfly, is not to flatter its abilities, but is simply telling the truth.

Because many areas in Canada are inaccessible by any other transport means, rotary wing aircraft have filled the need in an ideal manner. Since they came into use, many mining and hydro projects have been completed which might otherwise never have been possible. Rotary wing aircraft are being used with increasing frequency for search and rescue operations, often accomplishing missions over water or land areas where other means of transport, by air, land or water, could never operate.

When floods have swept unhampered over the countryside, thousands of persons have been rescued by means of rotary wing aircraft, and without such a modern aid many of the people saved would undoubtedly have perished. Shipwrecked sailors off the shores of Canada have already been saved by the hundreds from vessels being battered to pieces on gale-swept and rock-bound shores, or from disabled ships drifting helplessly at the mercy of a raging storm. Working under terrific risk from weather conditions, Canadian search and rescue pilots have guided their helicopters on such rescue work when all other methods have failed.

Even when lifeboats, manned by experienced and hardy seamen, have been obliged to give up against tremendous seas the helicopters have gone out to hover over the stricken ships and save their crews. Making trip after trip they have picked up every man aboard, doing so by means of equipment suspended beneath the aircraft and designed to hold one or more men at a time.

The majority of airports which now serve large cities are usually miles away from a city centre. Ground transportation to and from them by bus or private automobile often takes hours because of the distance to be traversed and because of congested highway conditions. Eventually helicopters will take over the major transportation jobs of this nature, and will remedy the difficulty by speeding people between cities and airports. They can do so in a matter of minutes instead of hours. Thus another transit annoyance will be remedied, one which airline passengers at present are unfortunately so often obliged to face.

In Canada there are now two major flying companies who specialize in the operation of helicopters, who do not own aircraft of any other type. One of them is Okanagan Helicopters Limited of Vancouver, the other Associated Helicopters Limited of Edmonton. Both firms carry out similar operations, and some truly remarkable undertakings have resulted by such work. The former company has the distinction of being the largest private operator of helicopters in the world, and their activities in connection with flying contracts have taken their pilots and machines to all parts of Canada.

As examples of how these companies are aiding the progress of industry, a few of the projects undertaken will suffice. They draw a picture as a whole in connection with rotary wing aircraft operations which are increasing, actually as well as literally, by leaps and bounds.

The huge Alcan aluminum plant project at Kitamat, B.C., with its accompanying massive hydro plant at Kamano, B.C., now fully completed, were originally surveyed by use of Okanagan Helicopters' aircraft. The subsequent transportation of tons of equipment and hundreds of personnel to various isolated areas connected with the work was a major undertaking.

Topographical and geological surveys for Provincial and Dominion governments have been carried on for some time throughout Canada, and there is still an immense field to cover in this respect.

On the eastern side of the continent, officials of the Federal Department of Fisheries have been transported by helicopter to remote or isolated outposts in Newfoundland. Innumerable emergency and mercy flights have also been handled throughout the Dominion for the Department of Public Health.

A major geographical survey to date, carried out for the Canadian Department of Mines and Technical Surveys, was undertaken in the Arctic in 1955. Okanagan Helicopters handled the job, and as it is a typical Canadian endeavour of outstanding worth, a brief outline of what took place is of interest.

Two large Sikorsky S55 helicopters were first flown to Malton airport, near Toronto, where they were partially dismantled and placed aboard one of the R.C.A.F.'s big C119 "flying boxcars." By this means they were flown to Resolute Bay which is on the Arctic Circle in eastern Canada. Supplies and personnel taking part in the work were flown in by ordinary air transport by R.C.A.F. pilots and aircraft. The survey work was handled by government teams consisting of ten geologists and ten assistants.

Three additional bases were set up, one being located on Oksey Bay, on the southwest coast of Ellesmere Island, another on Eleff Rignes Island and the third on Melville Island. The geologists then went to work in earnest and were transported by helicopter to innumerable parts of the islands being surveyed. The main object of such work was to obtain accurate information about the areas of which so little was known.

The entire undertaking occupied the period from June 15, to September 15, 1955. Approximately 30,000 square miles of territory was surveyed in that time, which under old-time methods would have required the staggering period of twenty-five years to complete!

Over 5,000 pounds of geographical specimens were collected and later flown out to the department's headquarters at Ottawa. Study of them reveals accurate knowledge of the land structures of the Arctic islands from which they came.

When winter conditions manifested themselves, the survey was brought to a close, men and helicopters then being flown back to Toronto the same way they had gone north, by means of R.C.A.F. aircraft and flying boxcars.

In the not-too-distant future, large passenger-carrying helicopters will take over some of the jobs now being handled by highway buses. People who read through these pages will in the years to come enjoy the opportunity of riding comfortably in a bus-type helicopter. It will be as safe and probably much safer than on the busy highways.

A splendid example of the aerial buses, which will be commissioned for use in Canada in the near future, is the Fairey Rotodyne. Made in England by the Fairey Aircraft Company Ltd., it embraces the combined good features of a propeller-driven aircraft and a helicopter. It is the nearest thing to a flying bus yet developed. It is able to lift itself straight up from a takeoff point, which can be the roof of a building or the confined space of a downtown area in a big city.

Once it has climbed vertically to a suitable altitude, by the use of its huge four-bladed rotor, the two engines which operate forward propellers are set in motion, and the Rotodyne then surges through the air to its destination like a regular airplane. At its journey's end, the propellers are stopped and the craft slows to a stop in mid-air, being kept aloft by the revolving rotor which is slowly reduced in revolutions to lower the machine straight down to the ground.

Two stubby wings protrude from each side of the Rotodyne's fuselage, their duty being chiefly to hold the two propeller-driving engines. Throughout an entire flight it is the huge rotor which imparts most of the lift needed for the aircraft to be flown. Retractable wheel landing-gear enables the aerial bus to make much better forward speed than if the landing-gear remained down.

Okanagan Helicopters Limited plan to have one of these unique Rotodyne's in service by the end of 1960. It will shuttle back and forth many times daily over the Gulf of Georgia between the cities of Vancouver and Victoria, keeping to a regular bus-like schedule.

Its load capacity will be from twenty-five to thirty passengers, and it is expected that, once in service, it will become so popular as a time-saver between the two cities the demand will be for additional Rotodynes to handle the rush of traffic over the route.

It should be fully understood that rotary wing aircraft are not taking over work previously done by conventional types of airplanes. They have entered and established a completely new field of endeavour in aviation progress. As time marches on their use will in all probability become one of the greatest factors for world well-being, irrespective of the wonderful progress which is still in the future with the full development of rocket and atomic-powered aircraft.

Part seven / AND SO TO JETS

37. Translations of Jet Talk

JET ENGINES, AS APPLIED to airplanes, are not yet very old in years, and many of the definitions used in relation to them, and particularly in conjunction with the aircraft which they propel, are unintelligible to many people who read about them. A full description of all such technical details is not in mind here, but there are some definitions which should be made clear for all who wish to know.

How to Spot a Jet

Providing the weather is clear and visibility good, it is quite easy to spot a speedy jet as it wings past overhead or in the distance, if you know how.

The sound waves A reach your ears a considerable distance behind the actual place in the sky where the jet is flying at the same moment. It is approximately at B. The aircraft is flying so fast that the sound from it does not come directly to your ears.

To locate the jet, listen carefully to learn the direction in which the sound waves are moving, do not look haphazardly for the jet itself. When you have decided which way the sound is moving, look a long way ahead, straight forward from where the sound is reaching you. You look towards point C. Then slowly search the sky back towards the sound waves you can still hear, and the aircraft will soon be spotted.

It will astonish you sometimes how far ahead of the sound the jets are. The distance depends on the height they are flying, and the speed at which they are travelling.

THE MYSTERY OF MACH.

The definition of the word Mach needs also to be dealt with. In the layman's mind there is much confusion as to its actual meaning and its correct pronunciation, and the explanations which follow will eliminate such mysteries. Once the facts have been read, and grasped, it will be a pleasure to discuss with others, what is meant by breaking the sound barrier, or to explain to people not so well versed just what is the meaning of Mach.

One day I was walking past a city school playground, and I was attracted to the noise coming from a number of boys, who were running in line pell-mell across the area, yelling "Mash one, mash two, mash three," and doing so at the pitch of their voices.

It was a game I had never played when I was at school, and as I went my way I was quite mystified. Thinking it over later, it suddenly came to me that the kids were of modern type and that they were playing at being jet pilots, or maybe spacemen.

The "mash" the young fellows were hollering about was in reality the word "Mach," and they were unconsciously pronouncing it incorrectly.

The name Mach stems from the name of the Austrian scientist, Professor Ernst Mach (pronounced MOCK), who was the discoverer of shock-vibration waves moving through the air, caused by the passage of a solid object through the air at a high velocity.

When an aircraft causes the noise described as breaking the sound barrier, it is because it has reached the speed of sound and it is then that the shock sound waves are set up.

In the realms of supersonic airplanes, an instrument bearing Mach numbers, starting at one, has replaced the conventional instruments which ordinarily measure speed in miles per hour.

Every test pilot or other airman who climbs aboard a jet capable of a speed of more than 760 miles an hour, *which is the speed of sound*, must have an instrument to record such velocity and the Machmeter was invented to fill such a need. A dial marked in miles an hour would be useless. Remember, it is pronounced, Mockmeter.

The Machmeter dial, is marked out in numbers beginning at zero and increasing in decimal points to one and then, again in decimal readings, to two, and so on. Whatever the figure the indicator points to in supersonic flight that is referred to as the Mach speed through the air of the aircraft. When the indicator reaches the number one on the dial, it means the aircraft has reached the speed of sound, or in other words, 760 miles per hour.

Although very few manned airplanes have yet reached the speed of Mach Two, twice the speed of sound, and the tremendous velocity of 1,520 miles an hour, some have, and it is only a matter of time before most military aircraft will be ripping along in the stratosphere at such enormous speeds.

Bang Goes the Sound Barrier

The above words, or "supersonic speed," and maybe the expression "faster than sound" are all terms we are quite familiar with if we read the newspapers or articles dealing with aviation. Such phrases read all right, but they do not divulge much in respect to their actual meaning.

When an airplane is flying it sets up vibratory sound waves which spread out in all directions in the surrounding atmosphere. These waves travel at a speed of 760 miles an hour, because that is the speed with which such vibrations are able to travel through the atmosphere.

As the waves of sound move much faster than an airplane flying, for example at 600 miles an hour, they cannot be "caught up" by the aircraft, because they are travelling at 760 miles an hour and proceed well ahead of the machine.

A very different thing takes place when an airplane reaches the speed of 760 miles an hour, the speed of sound. The vibrationary sound waves which before travelled ahead of the airplane are now caught up with and things begin to happen, because the airplane is travelling at exactly the same forward speed as are the vibrations.   The waves have no time to smooth themselves out in the surrounding atmosphere and, as the ship drives forward into the air turbulences caused by itself, a tremendous resistance is set up.   For a few moments, as it passes through them at increasing speed, immense strains are imposed on the airplane.

It is at the speed of 760 miles an hour that an airplane is said to have reached the sound barrier, although in reality it is contesting the enormous air upheaval it has caused itself.

Sound waves, so called, are actually vibratory waves which the human ear picks up as sound.   When a jet airplane, or a rocket missile, smashes through the sound barrier, the noise it makes comes to our ears as an explosion.   The pilot hears nothing although he knows full well what is taking place from the rough actions of his machine or a glance at the Machmeter.

Once the speed of sound has been reached and passed by a plane, the vibratory turbulence ceases because the aircraft is rushing forward into smooth air as the disturbed air is left behind.

If you have watched a waterborne ship ploughing its way through water, you may have noted that its bow causes a wave which spreads widely after the boat has passed.   Sound wave vibrations act in a similar manner in the atmosphere, except that they spread out in all directions, and at a far greater velocity.

As we stand on the ground, the sound of a passing airplane reaches us just as the wave from a ship might reach us, if we were standing at the water's edge along the shore.

When an airplane smashes against the turbulent sound waves it has set up ahead when reaching a speed of 760 miles an hour, the sound reaches us as an explosion as it sweeps past our ears.

As a jet retards its forward speed, say from 775 miles an hour down to 700, there is no noise as it drops back through the 760-mile-an-hour sound barrier mark.

The reason is simple.   As the speed diminishes, and it retards from 761 to 759, the sound waves switch from the rear of the plane to the front and, as the plane is not then catching them up, no tremendous sound or vibratory resistance can result.

Study the following diagram:

When an airplane, A, reaches the speed of sound, it is travelling at a speed of 760 miles per hour (Mach 1), and it is then referred to as "breaking the sound barrier." As it hits that exact speed in flight, a tremendous turbulence is created by the resistance of the machine against the air, and the vibratory waves, B, spread out in all directions. (For clarity, vibrations are shown in illustration from aircraft to ground.)

The vibratory waves, B, reach the ears of human beings as sound. Because the sound is travelling forward at the exact speed of 760 miles per hour, the same as the aircraft, the tremendous roar of the vibratory waves pass our ears, C, in an instant, leading us to believe we have heard an explosion. In reality, the sound is one continuous roar, sweeping past our ears at tremendous speed, from the direction of D to E.

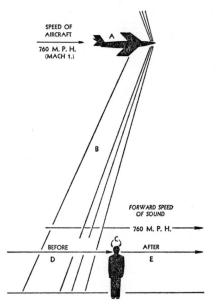

38. A Jet for One
—A Jet for Two

SINGLE JET-ENGINED fighter aircraft, De Havilland built, Vampires were the first jet type of airplane to be adopted for service with the Royal Canadian Air Force. They are single seaters, and they came into use shortly after the end of World War Two. Many Canadian military pilots have since graduated to them from propeller-driven machines, and the transition to much faster flying Vamps is always a great adventure.

They are capable of whipping along at a top speed of 550 miles an hour, so they are not sluggards by any means and an airman has to be well briefed in their operation before he takes over their controls in actual flight. The reason is that the Vampires are single seaters and, once a pilot is commissioned to fly one, he is entirely on his own.

With the advance in jet airplane design which has taken place so fast since the Vamps were originally placed in service, more modern jets have taken their place as first line of defence fighter aircraft.

Most of the Vampires now in use with the R.C.A.F. have been diverted for use by pilots belonging to the R.C.A.F. Reserve, who belong to what is termed the Auxiliary Air Force. It is composed chiefly of pilots who are now occupied in civil occupations, but who wish to keep their hand in at flying, and do so at weekends when they are able to get away from their workaday world.

SILVER STARS

Also known in Air Force vernacular as the T-33, the Silver Star is a more recent addition to military use in Canada than the Vampire. It is not a fighter type, but is used exclusively as an intermediate trainer in which pilots graduate from propeller-type airplanes to an advanced type of military jet fighter. In this jet an instructor is enabled to fly with a student and the consequent speed-up of training is greatly facilitated.

Silver Stars are frequently seen in the sky in many parts of Canada on training missions, and although they are not nearly as fast as Sabres, or the CF-100 Canucks, they certainly are not slowpokes when on the move.

Trim looking in their gleaming all-metal construction, they can make 580 miles an hour, and when a pilot graduates from flying one he has no delusions that he had not been in control of a fast and modern airplane.

Two wing-tip fuel tanks, in addition to the inside-the-wing fuel tanks, give the Silver Stars a flying range of almost 1,400 miles nonstop. It is understandable, therefore, that long-distance navigational flights may easily take a Silver Star, say from Winnipeg to the Pacific Coast, or from Montreal to Manitoba, in a single hop.

That is the kind of advanced flying training all full-fledged military pilots must have before they are finally put in charge of one of the latest and fastest jets the R.C.A.F. has in service.

The one-section protective plexiglass canopy, which locks firmly in place over the top of the two cockpits, gives the airmen wonderful visibility in all forward and side directions, making the Silver Star one of the safest jets now in operation in that respect.

Pilots who fly them are unstinted in their praise of the craft as a whole and, unlike the Vampires, it is probable the Silver Stars will be seen in our skies for years to come.

39. Flashing Sabres

IN DAYS OF OLD when knights rode into combat, dressed in gleaming metal armour, they fought fiercely and with bravery. Their flashing sabres clashed against shields and shining steel until one combatant became the victor.

Today, our fighting airmen stand just as ready to do battle with an enemy, but what a difference in methods. The flashing sabres are swords of steel no more, but instead they are beautifully designed aircraft. Equipped with guns and missiles, a single Sabre could cause more havoc in seconds than a vast army of men could have accomplished in weeks in ancient times.

Within the interior of a Sabre jet's body is installed a single Canadian-built Orenda jet engine, and it fits in so snugly together with all of its accessories that scarcely air space remains. There is room for only one pilot in the Sabre, because it is designed strictly as a fighter aircraft, not a bomber.

When the construction of these jet airplanes began in Canada, in 1949, it became the job of the Canadair Company at Montreal to produce them in numbers, and they did a splendid job. One thousand eight hundred and fifteen of the sleek-looking craft have been turned out at that plant, and many of the Royal Canadian Air Force Fighter Squadrons in Canada and overseas were early equipped with Sabres, whose pilots freely admit they are wonderful airplanes to fly.

There is an ancient motto, "In time of peace, prepare for war." It is the only sensible procedure for any nation to follow, because false security can well bring disaster to those who indulge in it. So the Sabres and their pilots stand guard in Canada and in many other parts of the world as well.

Squadrons of Canadian-built and Canadian-manned Sabres are stationed at many strategic points in Europe where they carry out daily exercises to keep them fit and ever alert through the uneasy peace which reigns over the world as things stand today.

The job of an R.C.A.F. pilot is a profession equal to any sought by a young man fresh out of school, or university. It is work of their own choosing, and they like it. They have a splendid opportunity of seeing the world at the same time, and a fellow can do a whole lot worse by following some other vocation. The comradeship which exists between the men of the air seems just a bit closer and more sharply defined than you may find elsewhere.

The Sabres they fly are each powered with a single Canadian-built Orenda jet engine, which imparts tremendous forward thrust to the machine. Once airborne, a Sabre can climb absolutely straight up and in a single minute can reach an altitude of 7,500 feet. Every minute as it hurtles upward another 7,500 feet is added to its altitude, until its ceiling is reached at 45,000 feet. The term, ceiling, is the ultimate height that any particular airplane is able to reach. The manner in which a Sabre can climb and disappear into the heights above takes your breath away if you are a mere spectator.

In level flight it is very fast. It can coast along at 600 miles an hour with ease. Should the occasion demand, the pilot can turn on the power and 760 miles an hour, the speed of sound, is soon left behind in its wake.

When a Sabre goes past in flight, high in the sky, it may be difficult for an uninitiated ground observer to catch sight of it in clear weather. They do not stay in one's vision for long in any case before distance and the great vault of the sky swallows them up.

So that readers may overcome this trouble when trying to locate a fast-flying jet of any type, a pictorial explanation has already been given in Chapter 37. Study it, and the next time a jet whips past, you will have a good chance of spotting it.

Once the method is mastered—and it is quite simple—much more enjoyment will be registered when you look for a jet as it howls by. It may be a Sabre and, if you are fortunate, it may be a whole formation of them, flying wing tip to wing tip as they come into your vision in grand array to sweep past and vanish into the distance almost as fast as it can be told.

40. Canuck, A Name
to be Envied

CANUCK IS A MAGIC WORD, and one which young Canadians should be proud to hear when it is applied to them. It is a definition frequently used to describe a Canadian by people of other nations and usually, when it is used, it is in terms of admiration. No other name could possibly be more appropriate when used in christening one of the latest twin-jet military airplanes produced in Canada.

The fast machine, described officially as the Avro CF-100 Canuck, has already earned the envy of other nations because of its splendid performance in the air. Without doubt it is conceded to be the fastest thing of its kind, in respect to its duties as an all-weather, night or day intercepter-fighter.

Since flying first began in 1903, a multitude of airplanes, made by many companies, have been allotted interesting names, some of which, like the Canuck, have become known the world over. Private owners also have done the same thing, and thousands of romantically sounding names have been given to individual airplanes since the Wright brothers' airplane of 1903— the first machine to fly anywhere in the world—was given the name of the *Kitty Hawk Flyer*.

The name of Kingsford-Smith's tri-motored monoplane, the *Southern Cross* is a byword in air history as the first airplane to fly across the Pacific Ocean. And who does not recollect the famous

217

Winnie Mae, flown by Post and Gatty on the first quick journey around the world by air? There have been many, many others. The list is legion.

It certainly does seem a suitable method of naming airplanes, instead of just giving them a stuffy old number. Such an airplane stands out beyond others which are nameless, just as a ship does. Once known, the name sticks in the memory, and that particular airplane is a nonentity no more. So the CF-100 becomes easily remembered as the Canuck, as does the world-famous F-86, when it is referred to as a Sabre.

The Canuck is capable of flying very much faster than 650 miles an hour-plus, which is the government method of giving out its air speed. The exact miles an hour has not been divulged, but the way it can break the sound barrier when desired, makes it no secret that it can travel at speeds far in excess of 760 miles an hour.

When a Canuck climbs into the sky in a hurry, its pilot can really put on a spectacular vanishing act. If he wishes, he can stick the nose of the twin-jet craft straight up to the heavens. Turning on the power, the jet leaves the earth behind at 12,000 feet a minute. Think of it, 12,000 feet a minute, that is over two miles, straight up, in sixty seconds! And the Canuck weighs over seventeen tons!! It is hard to imagine the tremendous power thrust generated by the two Avro-built Orenda jet engines, which together can impart such a violent impulse.

Although the Canuck seats two highly-trained pilots, and its fuselage is packed full to every available square inch with mechanical equipment, it is not a particularly large-sized craft. Its over-all measurements prove this. It is 52 feet from wing tip to wing tip, just about the width of a suburban lot, on which most homes are built. Its length is very much the same—54 feet 8 inches—from its rounded nose to the tip of its tail.

Added to its fine performance in the air, in speed and climbing ability, the CF-100 can fly nonstop for 2,000 miles, starting off with fuel tanks filled to the brim, and that is the way they always begin a patrol when taking off from an Air Force base.

The Canuck is the brain child of the Avro Aircraft Company, and is built in their massive plant at Malton near Toronto, where thousands of Canadians skilfully have worked on its production.

The machine was designed specially to fill the need for an aircraft intercepter fighter, and it is armed to the teeth with guns and air-to-air missiles, together with sonic-radar detecting devices which can spot an enemy plane in all weathers, and at night.

It is able to operate under the toughest of winter conditions, when temperatures drop to far below sub-zero readings, at the heights at which these special airplanes must fly on regular patrol.

The pilots who are trained to fly the Canuck are young men, keen and intensely interested in their work, many of whom have entered the Royal Canadian Air Force directly after completion of their education, either in high school or university. It is a splendid future to consider, which many young fellows should aspire to follow. Equal to most professions, and better than some, it is a job which holds good progress for advancement.

Then, too, the R.C.A.F. is not by any means a man's world. There are all kinds of responsible opportunities connected with its various branches, which are available to the women of the nation, who wish to enter the service. It is an interesting and remunerative life, filled with travel and adventure, which can form a fine future for any healthy Canadian boy or girl.

Of all the great fields of exploration which mankind has taken part in, none now holds a greater challenge than the air. Travel into the universe, beyond the earth's atmosphere, has not yet been achieved by man but we are on the brink of doing so, and time is running out before such flights will begin.

Some of the young people who read this book may, as they reach maturity, become members of some of the first manned rockets or atomic-powered ships which will flash out into space in search of adventure and scientific knowledge.

What is to be gained in the not-too-distant future, rests entirely on the ability and the shoulders of youth today when their turn comes.   It will be through their efforts that success in space travel will develop, a success which science has not yet succeeded in achieving so far as human flight is concerned.

How wonderful it must be to be young in an age which stands on the very verge of space travel.   Yes, it is thrilling indeed to realize that among the children of today some will become the men and women who will reach out into space in their beautifully built rocket ships to charter many routes to distant points which beckon so enticingly in the vast spread of the universe.

41. A Noble Scion, and the Whispering Giant

THE VISCOUNT

WHEN APPLIED TO A human being the title of Viscount means the owner is of noble birth. When the same definition is bestowed on an airplane by its manufacturers it conveys the same idea.

The Vickers Airplane Company of England designed and built the Viscount, a large commercial passenger airliner, fitted with four powerful Rolls-Royce turbo-jet engines. It is an imposing looking airplane, and as it is the first turbo-jet-driven aircraft for passenger-carrying to go into service anywhere in the world, the title of Viscount fits it well.

Capable of carrying forty passengers as well as a crew of five, it can travel at a speed of well over 300 miles an hour, as it cruises at a height of twenty-five thousand feet above sea level. Its roomy cabin, thirty-five feet in length and nine and a half feet in diameter, is pressurized so that the passengers feel no inconvenience and have no difficulty in breathing normally at a great altitude. People can thus travel at tremendous altitudes, where the rarified atmosphere outside the cabin contains insufficient oxygen to keep a human being alive. Pressurization inside the plane's interior allows the air surrounding its occupants to be kept at an exact ground atmospheric pressure, and the oxygen content the same as that which people are used to at such a level. It is controlled in this way by the use of suitable valves attached to

221

large oxygen tanks contained in the aircraft, and functions perfectly no matter at what height the airliner may be flying.

The wing span of the Viscount is almost one hundred feet, and the top of the huge rudder is twenty-six feet in height when measured from its peak to the ground when the aircraft is at rest.

Apart from its own net weight, the Viscount can lift an additional passenger-baggage load of four and a half tons, which brings its gross weight to thirty tons. The four turbo-jet engines, which rotate four four-bladed propellers, can drive the craft 1,700 miles nonstop before replenishment of fuel must be made.

The Vickers Viscount is of all-metal construction, and is quite impressive when seen on the ground or in the air. The first of these machines to go into service anywhere on the North American continent did so in Canada when they were acquired by the Canadian government owned Trans-Canada Airlines.

As this book is published, twenty-five have been commissioned for use and are operating over Canadian air routes, and to destinations in distant countries.

A Whispering Giant—The Bristol Britannia

The Bristol Britannia, a really huge aircraft, weighing 150,000 lbs., or seventy-five tons! Just think of it, seventy-five tons, speeding through the air as light as a feather, once it is airborne, and doing so at a top speed of 400 miles an hour, with a total of 133 persons seated in its spacious interior.

Yes, it is big, with its wing span of 142 feet, and length of 124 feet. Its vast rudder alone stands twenty-four feet high from its connections with the body to its high tip. Eight almost-man-sized wheels take the weight of the machine in landing, together with two additional nose wheels which come into use when the aircraft is fully on the ground. Fuel tanks with a capacity of 8,900 gallons enable the Britannia to fly nonstop almost 6,000 miles.

Operational performances like these were the influencing factors which caused Canadian Pacific Air Lines to order twenty-five Britannias for use along their long-distance air routes.

The four Bristol Proteus turbo-jet engines, each swinging a four-bladed propeller, develop a total of 16,000 horse-power. The engines, powerful as they are, run so smoothly and quietly that passengers experience absolutely no discomfort either from noise or vibration. That is why the Bristol Britannia so fully lives up to its flattering, and appropriate nickname, "The Whispering Giant."

The massive job of designing the machine in the Bristol aircraft plant, in England, can perhaps be grasped when it is divulged that it required the work of 300 draughtsmen to formulate the original plans, requiring the making of 40,000 blueprints.

To Canadian Pacific Air Lines goes the credit of obtaining and placing into service the first Britannias to go into service in the Western Hemisphere, the first of which were commissioned into use in 1958.

From their main base of operations at Vancouver, B.C., C.P.A.L. Britannias now fly nonstop to Tokyo over a direct route across the Pacific Ocean, while another route lies over the Polar Regions direct to Amsterdam to serve the European trade.

Flying in a "Whispering Giant," passengers can travel between Japan and Canada in double-quick time. They can step aboard at Tokyo and less than thirteen hours later can walk down the disembarking steps at Vancouver's International Airport.

Just think of it, only half a day to travel a quarter of the way around the world. It seems fantastic, but even faster time will result when the jet airliners come into full use. Speeds will be double what they are now, and then it will be routine to fly completely around the world in less than a day.

However, we are now dealing with actuality, and the turbo-prop jets have things to themselves at the moment. With their beautifully smooth operation, the Viscounts and the Britannias will certainly remain in use for many years before the advent of the true jet airliners influences air travellers to make use of them in the coming age which will demand speed and still more speed in accomplishing world travel.

42. Comets, and Conclusion

THE STORY BEHIND the Comet passenger-carrying airliners is one which has been world news since the first prototype was built in the De Havilland factory in England.

The original Comet I was hailed as a tremendous forward step in the design of large commercial airliners, and great were the accomplishments expected of it, over all propeller-driven aircraft.

Its first tests appeared to prove it to be an immediate success, and it seemed it was at once destined to lord it over conventional airplanes by reason of its superior speed and smooth-riding abilities. Its quiet vibrationless flight made it a dream aircraft come true, and apparently it was on the verge of revolutionizing air travel over many of the world's existing air routes.

But difficulties lay ahead which had been unforeseen. Due to a number of unfortunate accidents which destroyed some of the Comets, all others in operation were grounded for complete checks and additional tests before they could continue in use. So the remarkable advance they were expected to make was delayed for several years.

After lengthy and additional research, De Havilland designers and engineers finally ironed out the kinks which had plagued the originals, and the result was the sleek-looking jet airliner, Comet III.

Before its namesake, the Comet IV could be built in numbers, for sale to airline companies, the De Havilland people decided to put the craft to the severest tests possible, and one of their decisions was to have it make a trip around the world. They felt that as it accomplished such a journey it would have to undergo climatic, weather and other conditions which would be met by airplanes in general world use.

The Comet III, under the direction of the pilot, Captain John Cunningham, left England in 1955 on the first lap of its flight with Sydney, Australia, its first objective. From the antipodes the flight continued to Fiji, then to Honolulu, and so to Vancouver, British Columbia, its first touchdown in Canada.

The average cruising speed of the Comet III is over 500 miles an hour, and the pilot keeps the craft flying at an altitude of approximately 42,000 feet above sea level, because that is the height at which it operates most economically at full speed.

On every lap of the world journey the Comet III shattered existing times established by other airplanes over the same routes. As an example of its capabilities and speed, the trip from Honolulu to Vancouver, on December 16, 1955, covered the 2,780 air miles between the two cities in an elapsed flying time of five hours and thirty minutes. That is less than six hours to fly across almost two-thirds of the Pacific Ocean! With but one day's stopover at Vancouver the airliner continued its record-making progress, going on to fly nonstop to Montreal, right across Canada in a little more than four hours.

The De Havilland company had instructed the pilot and his crew not to intentionally endeavour to break records, as the entire flight was planned to follow regular airline routine. Nevertheless, with the superior speed the Comet possessed, it could not help but break record after record, no doubt much to its makers' satisfaction, in spite of their expressed precautions.

Another instance of its startling speed was the final lap, when the aircraft streaked from Montreal to London, England, overnight on December 27-28, 1955, in the time shattering record of six hours and eight minutes.

The successful completion of its world-girdling effort brought high praise of its capabilities from all quarters. The result of the findings of the flight was a new series of De Havilland airliners, the Comet IV, and they have since fully proved their capabilities without the shadow of a doubt.

It is probable that Comets will be commissioned into use in Canada because Canadian Pacific Air Lines hold an option to purchase a number if they finally decide to make use of them. Of course, cost of an airplane against operating income are the primary items which such large concerns must consider and, as the price of a single Comet IV is approximately $1,250,000, it requires careful planning and a thorough look into the future before final arrangements are made.

However, there is no doubt that the day will come when we shall see many propellerless jet-engined airliners in Canada and if you live in the vicinity of a busy central airport plenty of opportunity will present itself for you to see them in action. Not so the people who live along the routes the high flying jets will follow to their various destinations. Jet airliners will be at such great altitudes as they wing past overhead that the sound from their powerful engines will be lost in the distance. As for seeing them with the naked eye, the chances are practically nil.

The period in future air progress is not too distant when great changes will take place in respect to passenger air travel. First, the propellerless jets will take over and then they in turn will have to bow to defeat as rocket-powered aircraft pass from the experimental stage into commercial production.

So world progress moves forward. When the age of atomic power at last comes into its own, the rocket ships will probably be obliged to take a back seat. The ultimate in design may then perhaps have been reached, and space travel by man will have become an established fact, and to destinations at least as far away as the moon.

Index